EXTANT

MEDIEVAL

MUSICAL

INSTRUMENTS

EXTANT MEDIEVAL MUSICAL INSTRUMENTS:

A Provisional Catalogue by Types

Frederick Crane

UNIVERSITY OF IOWA PRESS
IOWA CITY

Library of Congress Catalog Card Number: 72–185993
University of Iowa Press, Iowa City 52240
© 1972 by The University of Iowa. All rights reserved
Printed in the United States of America
ISBN 87745–022–6

CONTENTS

ILLUSTRATIONS

vii

INTRODUCTION

Studies of the musical instruments of medieval Europe have been based almost entirely on indirect sources, iconographic and verbal. While account is sometimes taken of the direct sources—the extant instruments —they have not yet drawn enough attention to yield more than a tiny fraction of the information they offer. It is natural to assume that there are practically no medieval instruments preserved. One reason for such an assumption is that the important collections of instruments, which together contain a substantial number of sixteenth-century instruments, have not more than a dozen or two post-Roman, pre-1500 instruments. Most of the medieval instruments are widely scattered among art and archaeological museums. Many have never been published in the organological literature (or at all). Even the existence of some types is unknown to the literature.

The present list is offered to facilitate fuller use of the instruments themselves as sources. The list is strictly provisional, and makes no claim of completeness. In fact, the rate at which new instruments come to my attention leaves no doubt that the number presently known to me is only a fraction of the number that wait to be discovered. While I began a file of medieval instruments about fifteen years ago, I can not claim to have made more than a random search for them. My principal source has been published literature: books and articles on musical instruments, catalogues of collections, and a sampling of archaeological publications. I have collected some information from the objects themselves, particularly on a visit to museums in the Netherlands, France, and Austria in 1964. Personal communications have been particularly valuable, and have proven to be the best source of leads to new material. I am especially indebted to W. A. van Es of the Groninger Museum, and to G. Elzinga of the Fries Museum, for their painstaking inventories of the valuable instrument collections of those two museums. Among others who have been especially helpful are: Professor A. V. Artsikhovsky of the Institute of Archaeology of the University of Moscow; Dr. H. Brunsting of the Rijksmuseum van Oudheden, Leiden; R. Delagneau, Conservateur de the Musées de la Ville de Boulogne-sur-Mer; Miss M. H. P. den Boesterd of the Museum Kam, Nijmegen; Dr. Ernst Emsheimer of the Musikhistoriska Museet, Stockholm; Professor H. Halbertsma of the Rijksdienst voor het Oudheidkundig Bodemonderzoek, Amersfoort; the late Dr. Hans Hickmann of Deutsche Grammophon Gesellschaft; Professor B. A. Kolchin of the Institute of Archaeology of the Academy of Sciences of the USSR; J. V. S. Megaw of the Department of Archaeology of the University of Sydney; Dr. Monica Rydbeck and Göran Tegner of the Statens Historiska Museum, Stockholm; Dr. Walter Salmen of the University of Kiel; Miss Margot Schwarz of Langerwehe, Germany; Reidar Sevåg of the Norsk Folkemuseum, Bygdöy, Oslo; and Dr. Robert Warner of the School of Music of the University of Michigan for his careful and helpful reading of the manuscript.

Many of the publications that provided material for the catalogue are quite old, and correspondingly unreliable, particularly in showing a naive inclination to believe that the antiquities they report are older than they really are. Many instruments that were once claimed as medieval are now dated in the sixteenth or seventeenth century. A good case is that of the oliphants. A century ago, at the height of the Romantic passion for medievalia, they were generally dated to the time of Charlemagne, and several were claimed to be the very horn that Roland blew at Roncevaux (although their excellent preservation is proof that they could not be the instrument that Roland smashed on a Saracen head, according to the *Chanson de Roland*, laisse 170). Later they were attributed to the tenth or eleventh century, and now to the later eleventh century, mostly. It is easy to extrapolate, and show that by about the year 2400 the claim will be made that the oliphants do not yet exist. I have responded to the problem of dating by simply accepting the most reliable dating available to me. The best datings are based on well-founded archaeological evidence, or on the expert judgment of art historians. At the other extreme are many datings of very low reliability (usually indicated with a question mark).

In deciding what to include in the list, I have interpreted the criteria (extant, medieval, instruments) as liberally as possible. Some of the instruments are definitely not extant any more, and the present location of others is unknown, if they still exist at all. I have considered it sufficient that the instrument lasted long enough to be described or depicted as an object of some antiquarian interest. As a criterion for dating, the medieval period is considered to extend from the Migration Period (ca. A.D. 400) to ca. 1500. But, at the early end, I have included many instruments that are possibly older than the Migration Period, and a few that are certainly older. At the late end, a few instruments are included that may date from after 1500, while I have excluded instruments dated ca. 1500 that correspond closely to common sixteenth-century types. Finally, I have interpreted the concept "instrument" liberally, to include

x

musical instruments in the narrow sense, but also signal instruments and noisemakers, and even a few objects that might not have anything to do with sound production. In short, I have included anything that has come to my attention that might be a medieval instrument, preferring to include what may be excluded on the basis of better information, rather than to exclude anything that might prove to belong on the list.

In the case of a few types of instruments (bells, *rangler*, jingling ornaments, horn whistles), I have not attempted to compile a catalogue. All of these are quite numerous, but have been published only at random.

The list is intended, as much as anything else, to elicit information and stimulate investigation. I will particularly welcome correspondence correcting or supplementing information therein. The list can be taken as a status report on knowledge of the field, and on that basis I hope that many readers with access to the instruments listed or to others will publish fuller, corrected studies of parts of the material. For my part, I promise supplements, as new material accumulates.

Another object of the present publication is to aid in the identification of objects as musical instruments that may not now be recognized as such. For this reason (and for the sake of orderliness), I have listed the instruments by types, with a description of general characteristics and individual variants of each type, and a drawing of an example of most types.

The classification by which the types are organized makes no attempt to be complete or systematic. Its purpose is simply to organize the extant instruments according to types that can be readily distinguished. The outline follows roughly the classification of Hornbostel-Sachs (1914).

1. Idiophones
    11. struck idiophones
        111. bells
        112. rangler
        113. jingling ornaments
        114. ceramic vessel rattles
        115. scrapers
        116. cog rattle
        117. bell substitutes
2. Membranophones (none known)
3. Chordophones
    31. chordophones with strings mounted parallel to the surface of a flat resonating box
        311. kokle, gusli (without hand hole)
        312. gęśle, gusli (with hand hole)
        313. lyres and bridges
    32. plucked chordophones with fingerboard on neck
        321. bass zither

443. bovine horns

444. wood horns and mouthpieces

445. ceramic horns

446. glass horns

447. copper, bronze, brass horns

448. other metal horns

449. buisines

45. keyboard aerophones

451. organs

In the catalogue below, the three or four digits to the left of the decimal point identify each type of instrument, and the digits to the right of the decimal point identify the particular examples.

In naming the instruments, I have followed the well-chosen English-language terminology of Sibyl Marcuse (1964), with the exception of "bowed harp," her term for some of the instruments of my type 312. These are not harps, but instruments sharing lyre and zither characteristics.

The bibliographies that accompany the entries on most instruments are selective. Older and less informative sources have been omitted where better ones exist.

Special mention should be made of two unusually rich, but little-known sources of excavated musical instruments. One is the *terpen* (or *wierden*) of the provinces Frisia and Groningen in the northern Netherlands. The terpen were large mounds of earth raised by North Sea lowlanders as protection from floods, and inhabited by them from ca. 300 B.C. to the eleventh century, when dikes made them unnecessary. After about 1850, their soil was hauled away in most cases, at which time a number of antiquarians salvaged a rich collection of artifacts from them. Because of the lack of careful, modern excavation, very few of the objects can be dated, except to an uncertain time within the whole period of the occupation of the terpen, or possibly even later. The majority of the objects are in the Fries Museum, Leeuwarden, and the Groninger Museum voor Stad en Lande, Groningen, but others are in smaller municipal museums and private collections. The terp finds include more than half of the bone flutes and whistles in my list, about 18 ceramic vessel rattles, three ceramic whistles, and a number of unusual reedpipes. *Atlas van Nederland* (1960), Pl. IV, 1–2, shows the locations of the terpen; Boeles (1951) is a history and archaeology of the terpen; Roes (1963) is a particularly good source of information on the instruments.

The excavations in the Nerev end of Novgorod carried out in 1951–1962 produced virtually a complete record of the material life of that Russian city from the tenth to the fifteenth century. The musical instruments excavated include five gusli and a number of gusli fittings, four fiddles, two wooden duct flutes, a Jew's harp (as well as a sixteenth-century one), bells, and rattles. Artsikhovsky (1956–63) and Kolchin (1964) are preliminary reports on the results of the excavations, including brief notes on the instruments. Thompson (1967) and Zasurtsev (1967) are general reports on the excavations. Kolchin (1968), the first of a series of detailed publications of the finds, includes pictures and full descriptions of all the wooden instruments.

Many projects for future research on the medieval instruments can be proposed. A major need is for enlarging my list, by identifying new specimens, and even new types. For example, I have not located any object that I could identify as likely to be a clapper. But is is not unlikely that some bone or wood clappers have been excavated.

A much more thorough search of the archaeological literature than I have made would undoubtedly turn up more material. But a search of museums would be far more promising, because of the enormous amount of unpublished material they contain, and because the publications, particularly the older ones, often fail to identify the objects as musical instruments. An ideal museum search would not be limited to any period, but would aim at inventorying all instruments from the Paleolithic on.

Hardly any category of medieval instruments has had a thorough, careful study like those of Hans Hickmann (1949) of Egyptian instruments, Broholm, Larsen, and Skjerne (1949) of the lurs, or Coles (1963) of the Irish bronze-age horns. Such studies would be very welcome for any of the smaller or larger categories of pre-Renaissance instruments. Finally, the data provided by the instruments should be integrated with the iconographic and verbal data.

A number of special problems can already be defined. Why are no excavated medieval instruments reported from southern Europe? I do not know of a single one from Portugal, Spain, Southern France, Switzerland, Italy, Austria, or Albania.

It is interesting that the excavated instruments are mostly folk instruments—bone flutes, reedpipes, Jew's harps, rattles of various sorts—while those preserved above ground belong to the nobility, the church, and the professional musician. Does the preserved sample provide a good cross-section of the types that were in existence? Naturally, it is the more durable instruments (bone, ceramic, bronze) and those of greatest artistic value (a quality less fragile than musical value) that have been preserved. Many types (drums, instruments of reed and bark) have neither advantage, and have left no trace.

EXTANT

MEDIEVAL

MUSICAL

INSTRUMENTS

EXTANT MEDIEVAL MUSICAL INSTRUMENTS:

A Provisional Catalogue by Types

111. BELLS

Bells are preserved in great quantity and variety from throughout the Middle Ages and from all over Europe. Their number is so large, and their documentation so imperfect that I have made no attempt to catalogue them. Inventorying at least the larger bells is a very desirable project, begun for Germany with Grundmann (1959), which catalogues around 2,000 bells of the twelfth to nineteenth centuries; Åmark's work (1960) is a study of the Swedish bells of the Middle Ages.

The extant forms include pellet bells, bells of sheet metal formed and soldered or riveted, and cast bells of all sizes, in bowl, beehive, and sugar-loaf, as well as campaniform shape. Bronze is the predominant metal, but iron examples also exist. The smaller bells are mostly from excavations, the larger ones preserved in continuous use as church bells. There are also several bell-shrines from Ireland, richly bejewelled, in which were preserved the personal bells of various saints.

112. RANGLER

A rather common piece of Viking grave-goods is the so-called *rangle;* basically an iron loop, from which hang three to five oval or round iron rings (Fig. 1). Sometimes each of the rings has a smaller ring hanging from it. Many examples also have a sort of hollow handle attached to the loop, and a second handle, separate, but with a hook for temporary attachment to the loop. In some examples, fragments of rope attached to the handles are preserved, and others, instead of handles, have a chain linked at one end to the loop, at the other to a hook.

It is difficult to say just what was the function of the rangler. It is clear that they were intended to be hung and caused to jangle by some motion. The most convincing speculation is that they were horse trappings, with a function like that of the familiar sleigh bells. It is thought that they were intended for use in ritual processions, and it is probably significant that a large part of them come from warriors' graves. The rangler date from the eighth to tenth centuries, and practically all of them come from a small area on the southeast coast of Norway.

One hundred fifty-eight examples were known to Petersen (1917), who gives a typology and chronology of the rangler. See also particularly Brøgger (1917–28), II, 233–237, 348–349, and Rygh (1885), Nos. 460–467. Most of the rangler are preserved in the Universitetets Oldsaksamling, Oslo.

113. JINGLING ORNAMENTS

A variety of excavated objects can be assigned to a category of jewelry or other personal ornaments with loosely attached bells, rings, or other metal pieces intended to make a jingling noise with the body's motions. The examples which have come to my attention include bracelets with rings strung on them in the fashion of rangler (parallel also to the medieval and Renaissance form of the triangle), and pendants or pins from which dangle bells or variously shaped metal jingles on chains (Fig. 2). The latter objects are very common from Russia and the rest of Northeastern Europe in the earlier Middle Ages; some bear a remarkable resemblance to the *cimbalum* of some of the manuscripts of the *instrumenta Hieronymi* (see Hammerstein, 1959).

114. CERAMIC VESSEL RATTLES

A number of rattles of fired clay with pebbles or other hard objects loose inside are known from the Netherlands, Poland, and Russia, and there is little doubt that a search of museums elsewhere would turn up more of them. The terp examples, with the exception of No. 114.12, are similar in size and shape, varying between 4 and 9 cm. in maximum dimension, and varying among spheres, ovoids, and double cones in shape. Of the several Polish medieval ceramic rattles mentioned by Feicht (1962) and Kamiński (1963), I have seen specific information about only No. 114.19. Those excavated at Novgorod have not been published yet. I feel that these rattles are more likely to have served a magic or ritual use than to have been children's playthings.

114.01 Groningen, Groninger Museum voor Stad en Lande, 1884/I 79. Found in a terp near Loppersum, Groningen Province, Netherlands. Length 9 cm., diameter 5.5 cm. Ovoid, decorated with parallel longitudinal and circumferential lines.

114.02 Groninger Museum, 1891/VI 23. Found in the terp at Westerwijtwerd, Gem. Middelstum. Length 8 cm.

114.03 Groninger Museum, 1891/VI 24. Found in the same terp as No. 114.01. Length 6.5 cm., diameter 4.5 cm.

114.04 Groninger Museum, 1899/VI 16. From a terp in western Groningen Province. Spherical, 4 cm. diameter.

114.05 Groninger Museum, 1917/X 24. Found in the terp at Oostum,

Gem. Ezinge. Rounded conical shape, diameter 4.5 cm., height 3.7 cm.

114.06   Groninger Museum, 1946/V 59. Found between 1893 and 1906 at Toornwerd, Gem. Middelstum. Length 9 cm., diameter 6.2–6.4 cm.

114.07   Leeuwarden, Fries Museum, 14F–94. Found in 1905 in a terp at Bilgaard, Leeuwarden, Frisia Province, Netherlands. Length 9.5 cm., greatest diameter 5.6 cm.

114.08   Fries Museum, 22A–74. Found before 1900 in a terp at Stiens, Leeuwarderadeel. Length 6 cm., greatest diameter 4.5 cm.

114.09   Fries Museum, 25–141. Found in 1905 in a terp at Hijum, Leeuwarderadeel. Length 6.5 cm., greatest diameter 4.9 cm.

114.10   Fries Museum, 26–55. Found in 1870 in a terp at Hallum, Ferwerderadeel. Height 3.6 cm., diameter 4.7 cm. Conical, evidently half of a rattle.

114.11   Fries Museum, 27AA–52. Found in 1870 in a terp at Hallum, Ferwerderadeel. Length 8.5 cm., maximum diameter 5.5 cm.

114.12   Fries Museum, 28bis–111. Found in 1915 in a terp at Hoogebeintum, Ferwerderadeel (Boeles: Oosterbeintum). In the shape of a bird, with a separate head designed to nod as the rattle is moved. Height 10.6 cm., width 5.8 cm. See Boeles (1951), 204, and Pl. 36, No. 5. A Groningen bird-shaped rattle mentioned by Boeles is otherwise unknown to me.

114.13   Fries Museum, 31–2. Found before 1914 in Hanlum, Westdongeradeel. Height 8 cm., greatest diameter 7.3 cm. Mushroom-shaped, with perforations in the top like a saltshaker. Perhaps not a rattle.

114.14   Fries Museum, 40B–1. Found before 1929 in Hardegarijp, Tietjerksteradeel. Thickness 4.4 cm., diameter 7.1 cm.

114.15   Fries Museum, 45–131 (Fig. 3). Found before 1900 in a terp at Menaldum, Menaldumadeel. Length 7 cm., diameter 6.8 cm.

114.16   Fries Museum, 87A–48. Found in Frisia before 1918. Length 6 cm., diameter 4.4 cm.

114.17   Fries Museum, 136. Found in Frisia. Broken double cone. Present length 6.7 cm., diameter 5.4 cm.

114.18   Fries Museum, 143–45. Found in 1915 in a terp at Kubaard, Hennaarderadeel. Length 7.5 cm., diameter 5.3 cm.

114.19   Poznań, Muzeum Narodowe. A sphere about 3 cm. in diameter, decorated with hemispherical knobs all over, and a colored glaze. Kamiński (1968), 25, with Fig. XXII (photo with a reconstructed handle).

115. SCRAPERS

Only the first item in the list below can be called with full confidence a musical scraper, but its existence means that any object with a straight, serrated edge should be scrutinized for the possibility that it was intended

5

to be a noisemaker. Scrapers with sharp or delicate teeth are not likely to have been noisemakers, but rather utensils for scraping food, fibers or other soft materials. To make a sound, a hard, though not necessarily heavy, object must be rubbed against the notches. The likelihood that the scrapers had a ritual intent is particularly evident in the case of Nos. 115.3–5.

115.1 Wrocław, Instytut Historii Kultury Materialnej. Wooden scraper of the first half of the twelfth century, excavated in Opole. Length 20.2 cm. Feicht (1962), col. 1386 and Fig. 3; Kamiński (1963), 556–557, with drawing; Kamiński (1968), 26, with drawing.

115.2 Leeuwarden, Fries Museum (Fig. 4). A bovine rib, notched on the entire inner curve. From a terp. Roes (1963), 48, and Pl. XLIII, No. 4 (four other scrapers in the plate are less likely to have been noisemakers).

115.3–5 Three Alemannic coffins of the Migration Period. Each is made of a section of a tree trunk, and has a notched ridge along the top. Veeck (1931), 16–17, and Pl. 2, Nos. 1–3 (1 and 3 from the cemetery at Oberflacht, 2 from that at Zöbingen).

116. COG RATTLE

This mechanized scraper is essentially identical to the familiar modern ones.

116.1 New York, Metropolitan Museum of Art, 54.160 (Fig. 5; acquired in 1954; in 1887 in the collection of Mme. Achille(?) Jubinal). A heavy wood rattle, from the monastery Escaladieu near Bagnères (Hautes-Pyrénées); presumably it served as a liturgical rattle (see the discussion under type 117). Gay dates it in the fourteenth century, Winternitz in the fifteenth or sixteenth century. Gay (1887), I, 492 (engraving); Norlind (1941), Pl. 15, No. 8 (after Gay); Winternitz (1967), 53, and two photos p. 52.

117. BELL SUBSTITUTES

Since at least the eighth century, it has been the practice in the Roman Catholic church not to sound bells during Holy Week—specifically, in present practice, from the *Gloria* of Holy Thursday to the *Gloria* of Holy Saturday. A similar practice is observed in the Eastern church. Commonly, the functions of the bells are filled during this time by nonmetallic substitutes.

The variety of such instruments, mostly invented or adapted specifically as Holy-Week bell substitutes, is very great. Most of the examples reported in the nineteenth and twentieth centuries are cog rattles of sizes up to much larger than usual, single boards struck by a hand-held or attached and freely swinging hammer, and large boxes or multiple boards designed to be struck by trip hammers or by freely swinging hammers as the whole apparatus is rotated. A number of instruments of the last type are often mentioned in the literature as medieval survivals, without the claim that the extant instruments themselves were made in the Middle Ages. The only surely medieval instrument I know of is the small one described below.

On the liturgical practice, see especially Löw (1950), and the literature listed there. On the instruments, Sachs (1930), 27–31, and the literature mentioned there are particularly useful. Several varieties of the instruments are illustrated in Bonanni (1723): Nos. 109–114, 117, 123, and 130 of the 1964 edition.

117.1 Leningrad, Hermitage(?), Basilewski collection. A twelfth-century(?) Italian(?) ivory instrument, with two broad rectangular blades decorated with scenes from the Passion, held by a handle attached to the middle, with figures of Sts. Peter and Paul. Presumably a hammer once swung from one side of the top to the other. Maskell (1905), 213, 423. Instruments of this type are usually made of wood. One is illustrated in Sachs (1930), 30, and two paintings of Pieter Bruegel show them in action as carnival-time children's toys: *Children's Games,* and *The Conflict Between Carnival and Lent.*

311. KOKLE, GUSLI (Without Hand Hole)

Two types of medieval string instruments peculiar to Northeastern Europe must be discussed together because of their great similarity in shape. In both types, strings are stretched in a plane parallel to the front of a relatively shallow resonating box, fastened to a stringholder at one end, and at the other fastened without a bridge to the small ends of pegs inserted from the back. The instrument and its resonating box generally diverge from the lower end to the pegholder. The strings usually increase in length as they decrease in pitch, so that the pegs from left to right are progressively farther from the stringholder (the order of strings from high to low is the opposite of that of the modern fingerboard strings). Usually the pegholder is cut off at a uniform distance above the pegs, thus diagonally to the axis of symmetry of the instrument. But in some post-medieval examples, the top is cut off approximately at a right angle to the strings.

The only essential difference in the two types is that Type 312 has an opening from front to back between the pegholder and the resonator. In Type 311, the pegs are usually located immediately above the resonator, and the hole is lacking.

The two types are played in different manners. Type 311 is held across the lap of a seated player, the front facing away from him, his hands at the two ends of the strings, and is played by plucking. Type 312 sometimes is held across the lap, but more commonly upright in front of the player, whose left hand is inserted through the hole from the back to stop the strings—usually with the fingernails or backs of the fingers, as far as is known. The right hand plucks the strings below, or, in most of the recent analogues, plays them with a bow.

The medieval instruments of the two types come from a fairly limited area: from Gdańsk and Opole in Poland, from Latvia, and from Novgorod in Russia. Instruments of Type 311 dating from the eighteenth to twentieth centuries are plentiful in ethnological collections, and come from Finland (kantele), Estonia (kannel), Latvia (kokle), Lithuania (kankles), Russia (gusli), and Byelorussia (husli). The recent instruments analogous to Type 312 more often have a shape closer to that of the lyre, with distinct arms supporting a perpendicular yoke. They are known from Wales (crwth), Finland (jouhikantele or jouhikko), Estonia (rootsikannel; tall-harpa to the Swedish population), and Western Siberia (the nars-yukh of the Ostyak or Khanty people, the sangkultap of the Vogul or Mansi).

The numerous articles and books on the two types include Andersson (1930), Arro (1931), Famintsyn (1890), Jażdżewski (1966), Väisänen (1963) and Vertkov (1963), passim. A fine depiction of a player of gusli of Type 311, dating from the end of the twelfth century or the first half of the thirteenth, is reproduced in *Archaelogy* 21 (1968), 133, and Darkevich (1967), esp. Fig. 5.

311.01–02   Riga, State Central Historical Museum of the Latvian SSR. Latvian, both with runic inscriptions. The first, with five strings, is illustrated in Arbatsky (1949–51), Pl. 45, No. 1, where it is dated in the twelfth century. Arro (1931), 160, calls them "uralt."

311.03   Moscow, Institute of Archaeology of the Academy of Sciences of the USSR, Novgorod inventory No. 6–7–1576. Excavated at Novgorod in level 6, dating from 1396–1409. The preserved fragment comprises the pegboard and the top of the resonator. It is uncompleted, lacking pegholes. By analogy to the other Novgorod instruments, it probably was to have four strings. Fir: 10.5 cm. wide. Kolchin (1968), 86, and Pl. 83, No. 1 (photo).

311.04   Moscow, Institute of Archaeology of the Academy of Sciences of the USSR, Novgorod inventory No. 6–8–1264. Excavated at Novgorod in level 6, dating from 1396–1409. Enough of the one-piece fir body is preserved to allow a confident reconstruction. The gusli have four pegholes, plus an extra hole outside the basic series, perhaps to convert to a five-string instrument. Length 35.5 cm., greatest width (at top) 8 cm., depth 3.5 cm. Kolchin (1968), 86, and Pl. 81, No. 2 (drawing of top and cross section), Pl. 82, No. 2 (photo).

311.05   Moscow, Institute of Archaeology of the Academy of Sciences of the USSR, Novgorod inventory No. 6–12–218. Excavated at Novgorod in level 6, dating from 1396–1409. The extant fragment comprises the pegboard and the top of the resonator. It is broken off at the fourth peghole from the left, but probably had no more pegholes originally. Kolchin (1968), 86, and Pl. 81, No. 4 (drawings), Pl. 83, No. 4 (photo).

311.06 Moscow, Institute of Archaeology of the Academy of Sciences of the USSR, Novgorod inventory No. 8–11–1262. Excavated at Novgorod in level 8, dating from 1369–82. Nearly all the one-piece body is preserved. Three pegholes are extant; undoubtedly the original number was four. Length 47 cm., original width at top about 11 cm., 4.5 cm. deep at resonator. Kolchin (1968), 86, and Pl. 81, No. 1 (top and cross section drawings), Pl. 82, No. 3 (photo).

311.07 Moscow, Institute of Archaeology of the Academy of Sciences of the USSR, Novgorod inventory No. 5–9–1178. A supporting piece of a gusli bridge, found in level 5 at Novgorod, dating from 1409–22. Wood: 6.5 cm. long. Kolchin (1968), 86, and Pl. 83, No. 9 (photo).

311.08–15 Moscow, Institute of Archaeology of the Academy of Sciences of the USSR, Novgorod inventory Nos. 5–10–250, 9–6–1787, 10–18–1409, 10–11–1914, 12–17–322, 12–14–426, 12–14–426, 12–14–1589. Eight tuning pegs for gusli, excavated at Novgorod in levels 5, 9, 10, and 12, dating respectively from 1409–22, 1340–69, 1313–40, and 1281–99. Wood: 4–5 cm. long. Kolchin (1968), 86, and Pl. 83, Nos. 5–8 (photos of four of them).

312. GĘŚLE, GUSLI (With Hand Hole)

The antiquity of these instruments, essentially lyres, among the Slavic peoples adds to the evidence that the lyre was a universal Indo-European instrument, and therefore older than the development of the branches of the original Indo-European people.

The two Polish instruments of the list below have been claimed as bowed instruments, particularly on the basis of their recent analogues. Whether they were intended for bowing, plucking or both must still be considered an open question. If they were bowed, they are, with Nos. 331.1–2, the oldest bowed instruments preserved.

312.1 Wrocław, Instytut Historii Kultury Materialnej. Excavated in Opole, Poland, in the 1950s, the gęśle dates from the third quarter of the eleventh century. The body is made of a single piece of linden wood: now 23.5, originally not over 30 cm. long, 4 cm. wide at the top, 1.2 cm. deep. The preserved fragment includes most of the body, but lacks its upper end with the pegholes, so that it is not known whether it had two or three strings. The bottom of the hand hole, however, is clearly evident. The soundboard and the lower attachment for the strings are also missing. Feicht (1962), cols. 1386–7; Hołubowicz (1958, 1959); Jażdżewski (1966); Kamiński (1963), 551–554, (1968), 20–21, all with illustrations.

312.2 Łódź, Muzeum Archeologiczne i Etnograficzne (reliable reconstructions are in the Muzeum Prehistoryczne, Łódź, and the Muzeum Narodowe, Poznan). Excavated in 1949 in Gdańsk. From between 1255–75. Length 40.3 cm., greatest width 12.2 cm. The five pegs and all but fragments of the soundboard are lacking. The body is of a single piece of linden wood. Darkevich (1967), 217; Emsheimer (1961); Feicht (1962), col. 1386; Jażdżewski (1950–51, 1951, 1966); Kamiński (1963, 1966, 1968); Simon (1950, 1957), Strumiłło (1951). Most of the articles have illustrations; some, however, show a faulty reconstruction with the strings over the (decorated) back of the instrument.

312.3 Moscow, Institute of Archaeology of the Academy of Sciences of the USSR, Novgorod inventory No. 14–21–1346 (Fig. 6). Excavated at Novgorod, in a level dating from 1238–68. The three preserved fragments allow a reliable reconstruction. This is the only one of the Novgorod gusli to have a hand hole at the top. The pegboard, carved with bird-head shapes, must originally have had nine pegholes. Pine: 85 cm. long, the greatest width originally was 19 cm., depth 7 cm.; the resonator walls vary in thickness from .6 to .7 cm. Kolchin (1968), 86, Fig. 77 on p. 87 (drawings), Pl. 82, No. 1, and Pl. 84, No. 3 (photos). A reconstructed drawing has been reproduced several times: Darkevich (1967), 217; Jażdżewski (1966), Fig. 15; Kolchin (1964), Fig. 9; Thompson (1967), 101.

313. LYRES AND BRIDGES

Seven Germanic lyres and seven bridges are known. The two instruments from Oberflacht have been mentioned in print quite often, as has the one from Sutton Hoo in its earlier reconstruction as a harp, but the other objects are a little less well known.

The German and British lyres are all quite similar in design, as far as the surviving portions show. The body is made of a single piece of wood (Nos. 313.01 and .03 of oak, .05 and .06 maple), except that Nos. 313.01, .02, .05 and probably .06 had a separate piece across the top to hold the pegs. The body is hollowed out for some distance into the arms, and the soundboard (held on with nails, at least in the cases of Nos. 313.01 and .03) extended over all this hollowed portion. Nos. 313.01, .03 and .05 each had six strings; the others may have had the same number of strings, but the published information is not clear about it. All the three German lyres, whose bodies were sufficiently well preserved, were rather long, straight, and narrow, although 313.03 had gently incurved sides.

The Norwegian instrument is rather different in design, approaching the tortoise-shell shape of the Greek lyres, with a convex back. Its body was also of one piece, and its soundboard (not extending over the arms) was held on by nails. It is not quite certain how many strings it had, but the number was most likely seven.

The bridges are not unlike modern ones, each having two side pillars ending below in flat surfaces to rest on the soundboard, and above supporting the crosspiece on which the strings rested. All the intact bridges have notches for six strings, except No. 313.14, for seven. Five of the bridges are of amber, one of bronze, and one of horn or bone. All the bridges of the preserved lyres are lost, and it is likely that they were of wood.

The principal study of the lyres and bridges is Werner (1954), where it is shown that in pre-Carolingian Germanic lands the lyre was primarily reserved for the nobility.

313.01 Berlin, Museum für Völkerkunde, IIc, 4530 (acquired 1894; destroyed in World War II). Lyre found in a nobleman's grave of the sixth or seventh century in the Alemannic cemetery near Oberflacht, Kreis Tuttlingen, Württemberg. Length 81 cm., width 17 cm. at bottom, 20 cm. at top. Oak body about 2.75 cm. deep. Oak soundboard about .4 cm. thick. Preserved complete except for strings, bridge, stringholder and (?) pegs. Pegholes for six strings. Copies are in the Carl Claudius Collection, Copenhagen, No. 2 (53), the Musikhistorisk Museum, Copenhagen (1911 catalogue, No. C58), the Musikhistoriska Museet, Stockholm, No. 46, Bachhaus, Eisenach, No. 204, the Heyer Collection, Cologne, No. 760a (since 1926 in the Musikinstrumenten-Museum of the University of Leipzig, No. 760a), and the Museum of Fine Arts, Boston (Bessaraboff, 1941, No. 225). See esp. Behn (1954), 151–152; Veeck (1931), 20, 130, 300, and Pl. 4B, No. 9; Werner (1954), 13–14. Photographs of the original are in Kinsky (1929), p. 31, No. 2, and Behn (1954), Fig. 197. The Boston copy is reproduced in Bessaraboff (1941), Pl. VIII, and Galpin (1911), Pl. 9, No. 1; the Claudius copy in Skjerne (1931), p. 23; the Stockholm copy in Norlind (1941), Pl. 93, No. 4; the Heyer copy in Kinsky (1912), 377; and an unidentified copy in Niemeyer (1955, "Germanische Musik"), Pl. 76, No. 12.

313.02 Stuttgart, Württembergisches Landesmuseum (the original and reconstruction). Found in 1846 on the right arm of a young nobleman in grave 31 (from the second half of the seventh century) of the Oberflacht cemetery. Preserved: four fragments and a drawing from 1846. A shallow cut in the back of the extant arm suggests that the lyre originally had a crosspiece from one arm to the other near the top. The reconstruction is undoubtedly wrong in several details, particularly the number of its strings (eight), and the fixed-bridge construction without tailpiece. Bruce (1970), 9, 12; Fremersdorf (1941–42), 136–137, 139; Niemeyer (1955, "Germanische Musik"), col. 1816, and Pl. 76, No. 15 (the reconstruction); Veeck (1931), 20, 130, 298, and Pl. A, No. 4 (the reconstruction); Werner (1954), 13–14.

313.03 (Fig. 7) Excavated in 1938 under the church of St. Severin, Cologne. The lyre lay on the right forearm of a probably Frankish nobleman, in a burial of the early eighth century. The preserved fragments (destroyed in World War II) were extensive enough to allow a confident reconstruction. The body, including the yoke, was of a single piece of oak. The belly was of maple, 1–2 mm. thick, and fastened to the body with bronze nails. To strengthen the yoke, a piece of wood with grain running across was glued to each side of the yoke, plywood fashion. The lyre was 51.3 cm. long, and 18 cm. wide at the top. It had six strings, and an iron tailpiece. Fremersdorf (1941–42) (with drawings and photos of the grave, the lyre and the reconstruction); Fremersdorf (1956), 18, 26, and Pl. 15, No. 1 (the reconstruction); Megaw (1968, "Earliest . . . Instruments"), 132 (photo of reconstruction); Megaw (1968, "Palaeo-Organology"), 352, and Pl. XVI, e (photo of reconstruction); Niemeyer (1955, "Germanische Musik"), cols. 1816–17, and Pl. 76, No. 16 (the reconstruction); Werner (1954), 12–13, and Pl. I (the reconstruction).

313.04　Abington, Berkshire, Museum. Excavated in 1933 in grave B42 of the fifth-century Anglo-Saxon cemetery at Abington, the grave possibly dating from before 450. The extant fragments consist of two bone facings, one for each side of the yoke of a lyre. It seems likely that such strengthening pieces would be necessary only in a lyre whose yoke was of one piece with the arms and body, and therefore was cut across the grain. The two pieces are 18.3 and 18.5 cm. long. Each of them preserves five pegholes; the photos do not make it clear whether there was a sixth or not. Bruce (1970), 8, 10, and photos Pl. V, a; Meaney (1964), 43 (on the grave, no mention of the lyre). Earlier, the fragments were tentatively identified as belonging to two harps; see Steger (1961), 61.

313.05　London, British Museum. From a ship burial excavated in 1939 at Sutton Hoo, East Suffolk, just east of the town of Woodbridge (a cenotaph, honoring a king of East Anglia not yet conclusively identified). From the first half of the seventh century. The preserved fragments consist of the yoke, with six pegholes, the upper part of the arms, some fragments of the body, and two gilt bronze plaques representing birds' heads. The yoke was joined to the arms by a tenon-and-mortise joint at each end; rivets to hold the joints are attached to the backs of the metal plaques. The body was presumably of one piece of maple; the pegs are of poplar or willow, evidently made for use with a tuning key. The arms were hollow for most of their length, and covered by the soundboard. A reconstruction, 74.2 cm. long and 20.9 cm. wide, was made for the museum by the Arnold Dolmetsch workshop, Haslemere. The principal study of the lyre is Bruce (1970); see also *Harp* (1969), and Rensch (1969), 29–30.

The Sutton Hoo instrument was originally reconstructed as a rectangular harp, and many discussions and photos of it in this form were published before the reconstruction as a lyre was made public in 1969. See

12

esp. Bessinger (1957–58); Bruce (1947–50), 441, 446–448, and Pl. II; Bruce (1950); Green (1963), 73, and Pl. XVI, a; Hayward (1954), 7; Megaw (1968, "Palaeo-Organology"), 333, 352, and Pl. XVI, d; *The New Oxford History of Music, III* (1960), Pl. V; Niemeyer (1955, "Germanische Musik"), col. 1817, and Pl. 76, No. 18; *Saxon* (1948), with several photos; Steger (1961), 53–62, and Pl. 33; Wrenn (1959); Wrenn (1963). Bruce (1947–50), Hayward, *Saxon* and Steger include photos of the fragments.

313.06 London, British Museum. Two bird's-head plaques and some fragments of maple wood, excavated in 1882 in Taplow barrow, Bucks, near Maidenhead, Berks, a nobleman's grave of ca. 620–40. The instrument was undoubtedly very similar to No. 313.05. See esp. Bruce (1970), passim, and Pl. VI, b; also Meaney (1964), 59 (description of burial, literature); *Saxon* (1948) (photo of the plaques); Steger (1961), 61; Wrenn (1963).

313.07 Bygdöy, Oslo, Norsk Folkemuseum (earlier Oslo, Statens Museum). From Kravik Manor, Nore, Numedal, Norway. Said to have been excavated, but the circumstances of its finding are unknown. Dated in the thirteenth or fourteenth century, or perhaps much later. Length 71 cm., width 27 cm., and about 10 cm. deep. The body was evidently all of a single piece. There are now eight pegholes, but the middle part of the yoke, with five holes, is a nineteenth-century restoration; it almost certainly has one hole too many, and the original number must have been seven. Engel reports three pegs still present, but since at least the time of Panum's report only one remains. The soundboard is missing, but the remains of nails that held it on are present. Andersson (1930), 178–180 (photo p. 179); Emsheimer (1966) (with particularly good photos); Engel (1883), 60 (with drawings); Galpin (1911), 5; Panum (1905–06), 14–15 (photo p. 15); Panum (1915–31), I, 85–87 (photo p. 85); Panum (1941), 96–97, and Fig. 84.

313.08 Amber bridge, excavated in 1967 at the site of an eighth-century amber factory at Elisenhof, Schleswig, on the estuary of the Eider River. Fragment: one pillar and about a third of the crosspiece; 2.3 cm. high, 1.9 cm. wide. Bruce (1970), 8, 10, and drawings Fig. 2, left.

313.09 Amber bridge, excavated as No. 313.08. Fragment: one pillar and most of the crosspiece, preserving five and a half notches; 2.1 cm. high, 2.8 cm. wide. Bruce (1970), 8, 10, and drawings Fig. 2, right.

313.10 Cologne, Römisch-Germanisches Museum, Diergardt collection, 932. Bronze bridge, with an extra crosspiece below the string-bearing one, and with pillars extended into animal heads; 3.7 cm. high, 5.3 cm. wide. From a Frankish cemetery at Concevreux (Aisne) in northern France. Niemeyer (1955, "Germanische Musik"), Fig. 4, No. 1; Werner (1954), Pl. II, No. 1.

313.11　　Utrecht, Centraal Museum. Amber bridge, found in Dorestad (Duurstede), Utrecht Province, Netherlands, and probably dating from the eighth or ninth century, at which time Dorestad was an important trading town; 2.5 cm. high, 3.7 cm. wide. Niemeyer (1955, "Germanische Musik"), Fig. 4, No. 2; Roes (1965), No. 141, pp. 45–46, and Pl. XIX; Werner (1954), Pl. II, No. 2.

313.12　　Utrecht, Centraal Museum (Fig. 8). Amber bridge from Dorestad, probably from the eighth or ninth century; 2.5 cm. high, 5 cm. wide. Niemeyer (1955, "Germanische Musik"), Fig. 4, No. 3 (not 4); Roes (1965), No. 140, pp. 45–46, and Pl. XIX; Werner (1954), Pl. II, No. 4 (not 3).

313.13　　Amber bridge found in a chieftain's grave of the middle or second half of the eighth century, in Broa, Halla, Gotland, Sweden; 2.5 cm. high, 4 cm. wide. Andersson (1930), 174–177, with Fig. 54; Niemeyer (1955, "Germanische Musik"), Fig. 4, No. 4 (not 3); Werner (1954), Pl. II, No. 3 (not 4).

313.14　　Stockholm, Statens Historiska Museum. Bridge excavated at the "Svarta Jorden" (Black Earth), on the island of Birka (Björkö), Adelsö Parish, Uppland, in Lake Mälar, Sweden. From before 1000, probably ninth century. Variously reported as bone or horn: 3.3 cm. high, 4.7 cm. wide. Notched for seven strings. Photo Emsheimer (1966), Fig. 1; Niemeyer (1955, "Germanische Musik"), Fig. 4, No. 5; Werner (1954), Pl. II, No. 5.

321. BASS ZITHER

This unique instrument of fantastic outline is called in the German literature a "Basscister," and by Winternitz a basslute. It is probably better to call it a bass zither, from its near identity, except in shape, to a number of Salzburg zithers that have practically the same string arrangement, except for single choirs. See Norlind (1936), 272–273.

321.1　　Vienna, Kunsthistorisches Museum, Musikinstrumentensammlung, A. 60 (from the Ambras collection). German, formerly ascribed to the fourteenth or fifteenth century, but dated ca. 1500 by Winternitz. Length 175.5 cm., width 56.5 cm., depth 19 cm. On the fingerboard: six double strings; off the fingerboard on the bass side: four double bass strings; off the fingerboard on the treble side: three single strings. Schlosser (1920), 59–60, and Pl. X, No. 60; Schlosser (1922), Pl. 8, No. 23; Winternitz (1967), 54, and photo p. 55.

322. GITTERN

As the study and depictions published by Remnant (1965) show, the British Museum's gittern (Fig. 9) is closely paralleled by representations in fourteenth-century art.

322.1   London, British Museum (purchased in 1963 from the collection of the Earl of Brooke and Warwick, Warwick Castle). Length 60.5 cm., width 18.3 cm., depth 14.5 cm. The body and neck are of a single piece of boxwood, richly carved with foliage and hunting scenes; the decoration dates the instrument about 1300–30. Four strings. Given by Elizabeth I to the Earl of Leicester, whose coat of arms is on the silver plate attached in 1578 by I.P. It was probably in this year that the gittern was converted to a violin; the belly and fittings are of the sixteenth century and later. A copy made in 1869 is in the Victoria and Albert Museum, London. *English* (1964–65); Galpin (1911), 23–24, and Pl. 7; Smoldon (1965), Pl. 23; Winternitz (1967), 23, 47–48, and three photos pp. 49–50.

323. LUTES
Two preserved instruments are of widely different dates and types, but both can be assigned to the class of lutes.

323.1   Corinth, Archaeological Museum, M.F. 10169(?) (Fig. 10). From the end of the tenth century or the beginning of the eleventh. Excavated in 1961 in the Byzantine section of Old Corinth. Total length 44.5 cm., greatest width 11.5 cm., depth of body 7 cm. The body and neck are made of a single piece of hardwood. Other than this piece, only the stringholder is preserved—a separate piece fitted into the lower end of the body. Anoyanakis (1965), the only publication known to me, identifies the instrument as a lute of the tanbūr type, with long neck and small body, on the basis of analogies.

323.2   Eisenach, Wartburg. Mandora or lute by Hans Ott, ca. 1450. Five double strings; side pegs; body evidently of one piece of wood, tapering smoothly into the neck. Reinhard (1960), Pl. 82, Nos. 1–2.

331. FIDDLES
Bachmann (1964) shows conclusively, I think, that the first evidence for the bow appears in Islamic and Byzantine territory at the beginning of the tenth century, though bowing may have originated in Central Asia; it does not appear in Northern and Western Europe until after A.D. 1000, but had spread all over Europe by the end of the eleventh century. Thus the earliest preserved bowed instruments date from a time when they were very nearly a novelty.

The seven medieval fiddles that have come to my attention show a little of the great variety of shapes so evident in depictions. They have very little in common, except that they presumably were played with a bow, and that all of those for which I have any information have bodies made of a single piece of wood. The one-piece construction is shared by virtually all medieval string instruments except harps; in this respect they find their closest modern relatives in the European folk instruments, as the art-music instruments have long had bodies constructed of several pieces.

331.1 Moscow, Institute of Archaeology of the Academy of Sciences of the USSR, Novgorod inventory No. 23–29–775. Found in a level dating from the years 1055–76, in the excavations of medieval Novgorod. Only a fragment is preserved, about 20 cm. long: an end of the resonator, part of the body projecting beyond the part once covered by the soundboard. Kolchin (1968), 87, and Pl. 81, No. 7 (drawings), Pl. 82, No. 5 (photo).

331.2 Moscow, Institute of Archaeology of the Academy of Sciences of the USSR, Novgorod inventory No. 17–19–859. Found at Novgorod, in a level dating from 1177–97. The body, of a single fir block, is preserved intact; other parts are lost. Length 41 cm., width 11.5 cm, depth 5.5 cm.; the walls of the back average .5 cm. thick. Three pegholes. Fiddles of the shape of Nos. 331.2, 331.3, and probably 331.4 are very common in medieval art. Essentially identical instruments of the eleventh to thirteenth centuries can be seen in Galpin (1911), Pl. 15, No. 1; and Bachmann (1964), Figs. 29, 32, 35, 36, and 59. Similar folk instruments are still common in Eastern Europe. Kolchin (1968), 87, and Pl. 81, No. 6 (drawings), Pl. 82, No. 4 (photo).

331.3 Moscow, Institute of Archaeology of the Academy of Sciences of the USSR, Novgorod inventory No. 9–9–1876 (Fig. 11). Found at Novgorod in the ruins of a house that burned down in May 1368. The body and belly are of fir; the body is preserved essentially intact; most of the belly is preserved: 30 cm. long, 10.5 cm. wide, 3.3 cm. deep. Three pegholes. Kolchin (1968), 87, and Pl. 81, No. 5 (drawings), Pl. 83, Nos. 2–3 (photos).

331.4 Moscow, Institute of Archaeology of the Academy of Sciences of the USSR, Novgorod inventory No. 8–12–874. Found at Novgorod, in a level dating from 1369–82. Preserved: pegboard and top of resonator: 9.5 cm. long, 4.5 cm. wide. Three pegholes. Kolchin (1968), 87, and Pl. 81, No. 3 (drawings).

331.5 New York, collection of Irwin Untermeyer (in 1967; ca. 1943 Vienna, Bondy collection; until 1930 Vienna, Figdor collection; still earlier Vienna, collection of E. Miller-Aichholz). Winternitz: North Italian, fourteenth century; Falke: North Italian (Milan or Vienna), end fourteenth century; Geiringer: French, ca. 1400. The body is of one piece of boxwood, heavily carved with a female lute player at the top, and animals, people, and foliage on the back. A Gothic rose covers almost the whole belly. The fiddle had five strings, with crosswise pegs like a violin's, now lost. Length 46 cm., width 9.5 cm. Falke (1930), IV, No. 125, and Pl. LXVII (front and back views); Geiringer (1943), Pl. XII, No. 1; Winternitz (1967), 23, 48, and three photos p. 51.

331.6   Berlin, collection of Robert Leibbrand (in 1920). Ruth-Sommer (1920), p. 53, whose photo and brief description are my only source of information, calls the fiddle "medieval." It has five strings, and its body, neck and pegbox are all of one piece of beechwood.

331.7   Bologna, Chiesa del Corpus Domini. This four-string fiddle of rather eccentric shape is preserved among the relics of St. Caterina de' Vegri (Bologna, 1413–63), who played it. Cervelli (1967), 19 (with photo), 28–29; Disertori (1938), with three photos.

332. VIOLA DA GAMBA

332.1   Haslemere, Surrey, Dolmetsch Foundation. According to *Tribute* (1949; with photo), made ca. 1475 by Hans Volrat. Lütgendorff (1922), II, 544, states that Hans Vollrat, according to documents, was active in Vienna as a maker of lutes in 1424 and 1436. Baines (1966), 17, 19, and Figs. 80–82, reads the signature as Hanss Vohar(?), and dates the instrument in the late fifteenth century or later. Length 112 cm. Six strings.

341. IRISH HARPS

Nos. 341.1–3 represent a distinct type, being similar in size, shape, and all essentials of construction, such as in the heavy willow soundbox and brass strings. All are well known, and have been studied more fully than most sets of medieval instruments. Rimmer (1964) dates the type from "roughly the fourteenth to the mid-sixteenth century," and it seems difficult to date any one of the instruments more precisely than that. All three are more or less extensively repaired and restored. The fragment of No. 341.4 bears no resemblance to the other three, and has in common with them only its Irish origin.

341.1   Dublin, Trinity College Library (Fig. 12). The so-called "Harp of Brian Boru" (King of Ireland 1002–14). Thirty strings (originally perhaps only 29). Many times altered and restored, most recently to something like its authentic shape by the British Museum in 1961. Armstrong (1904), esp. 55–63, with 4 pl.; Galpin (1911), 13, and Pl. 4; Harrison (1964), Fig. 70; Hayward (1954), 3, 10; Panum (1915–31), I, 91–92 (photo p. 91); Panum (1941), 106–107, with Fig. 91; Rensch (1969), 82–85, and Pl. 26, a; Rimmer (1964), esp. Pl. V, a. On the theft of the harp for ransom and its recovery, see the *New York Times*, March 26, 1969, p. 12, and April 19, 1969, p. 11.

341.2   Edinburgh, National Museum of Antiquities of Scotland. "Queen Mary's Harp." Thirty strings (one a late addition). Greatest length about 79 cm., greatest width about 46 cm. Armstrong (1904), esp. 168–183, with 9 pl.; Hipkins (1888), 3–5, and Pl. II; Rensch (1969), 86–89, and Pl. 26, b; Rimmer (1964), passim.

341.3 Edinburgh, National Museum of Antiquities of Scotland. The "Lamont Harp." Thirty-two strings. Greatest length about 97 cm. Armstrong (1904), esp. 159–168, with 4 pl.; Baines (1966), 64–65, and Fig. 383; Hipkins (1888), 7–8, and Pl. III; Rensch (1969), 86–89, and Pl. 27, a; Rimmer (1964), passim.

341.4 In the possession of W. J. Knowles in 1897. The string arm of a harp, found in 1896 or 1897 in the bog next to the crannog of Carncoaga, County Antrim, Northern Ireland. A single piece of wood 33 cm. long, 4.5 cm. wide, 2.5 cm. thick. At one end there is a peg carved at a right angle to the arm for attachment to the soundbox, and at the other end a hole for the attachment of the supporting pillar. Thirteen pegholes. The shape of the arm, with a gentle downward curve in the middle, corresponds closely to harp depictions of the twelfth and thirteenth centuries, and the number of strings is also reasonably consistent with these; otherwise, there is no basis for dating the instrument. Knowles (1897).

342. CONTINENTAL GOTHIC HARPS

Two surviving late medieval harps from the continent are similar only in the great elegance of their decoration.

342.1 Eisenach, Wartburg (Fig. 13). Made in Tirol in the second half of the fourteenth or in the fifteenth century. Supposed to have belonged to Oswald von Wolkenstein. Wood, with fine inlays of wood and ivory in geometrical designs and, at the top of the forepillar, nine flowers and the word "wann." Maximum length 104 cm., maximum width 32 cm., maximum width of soundbox about 13 cm., depth of soundbox about 4 cm. Twenty-six strings. The Bachhaus, Eisenach, has a copy (No. 234). Hefner (1879–89), III, 37, and Pl. 213–214.

342.2 Paris, Musée du Louvre (Gift of marquise Arconati-Visconti in 1892). French, first half of the fifteenth century. Ivory forepillar and stringholder, wood soundbox (evidently, everything but the two pieces of ivory is a restoration). The fleur-de-lis decoration indicates that it was made for a French prince; the letters AY repeated many times in the decoration have been variously interpreted. The decorations in the ivory parts also include scenes of the nativity, the adoration of the Magi, and the massacre of the innocents. Length 42 cm., width 23 cm. The 25 strings conform to the number given by Guillaume de Machaut in his *Dit de la harpe*. Beigbeder (1965), 78, and Fig. 75 (detail); Dufourcq (1946), 26 (photo); Koechlin (1924), I, 465, II, 437–438, III, Pl. CCIX; Kunz (1916), Pl. opposite p. 61; Maskell (1905), 361–364, and Pl. LXXX; Molinier (1896, *Musée national*), No. 116, p. 198; Rensch (1969), 89–90, and Pl. 27, b.

351. CLAVICYTHERIA

If the dates usually assigned to them are correct, two of the three oldest keyboard stringed instruments are clavicytheria.

351.1   London, Royal College of Music, Donaldson Museum (earlier Venice, Correr Collection). North Italy, second half fifteenth century. Height (without the later base) 149 cm., width 69 cm., depth at base 28 cm. Range C-g², with short octave. Hipkins (1888), 13–14, and Pl. VI; Hirt (1955), 293, and photo p. 292; Norlind (1939), col. 138 (with photo).

351.2   New Haven, Conn., Yale University Collection of Musical Instruments (on loan from the Belle Skinner Collection, Holyoke, Mass.; earlier in the Morris Steinert Collection). Ascribed to the fifteenth century, but very possibly from the sixteenth. A small instrument, enclosed in a heavy, rich cabinet, on the doors of which are paintings of angel musicians after Fra Angelico (1387–1455). Height of case 97 cm., width 71 cm. Range c-f², with short octave. Hirt (1955), 4, and photo p. 5; Skinner (1933), 18–20 (photo p. 19).

352. VIRGINAL
352.1   Perugia, Galleria Nazionale dell' Umbria(?) (in a private collection in Perugia in 1910). Inscribed ALEXANDRI PASII MVTINENSIS OPUS MCCCCLXXXXIII, but according to Boalch (1956), 83, "the genuineness of this instrument is widely doubted." In the five-sided Italian form.

411. JEW'S HARPS
As practically none of the early European Jew's harps are known to the organological literature, I have taken the opportunity to list all those I know of that have been excavated and that probably date from the sixteenth century and earlier. Some have been lost since finding, and a few certainly date from before the Middle Ages. Most of them, unfortunately, were not found under circumstances that allow reliable dating.

The known dates and the locations in which these Jew's harps have been found allow some conclusions about the early history of the instrument in Europe. It was widely known in the Roman period. (In addition to the European examples listed, two Jew's harps of Roman date, found in the Nile delta, were in the stock of the Cairo antiquities dealer Nahman in 1947.) The instrument was known throughout the Middle Ages from one end of northern Europe to the other. It was a personal possession sufficiently prized that several were buried with their owners in Anglo-Saxon Britain.

In the earlier centuries, bronze was the preferred material for Jew's harp frames. Later—after roughly the tenth century—most are of iron. The bronze examples are always cast, and frequently have been filed to shape or decorated with file marks. (Among all the early molds for casting bronze objects, are there any for Jew's harps?) The iron ones are usually identified as wrought iron. The tongues, always of steel, have normally disintegrated (likely many were broken off in use), except for traces of rust at the point where they were joined to the frame, or, in some cases, a small stub; rarely, nearly the whole tongue is preserved. The form of the instruments is in no way different from that of the modern ones; the Jew's harp may be the only instrument manufactured in Europe today in a form that has been unchanged for two thousand years. The early instruments are generally small, commonly about 5 x 2.5 cm. or a little less in maximum dimensions.

411.01 Lullingstone, Kent, collection of G. W. Meates (in 1955). "Found in a post-Roman deposit at the Barn, Lullingstone." Bronze: length 3.9 cm., width 2.2 cm. One prong broken off .7 cm. from the end. Grove (1955), 212, and Fig. 4.

411.02 Guildford, Surrey Archaeological Society Museum. Excavated 1906 in a Saxon cemetery at Hawks Hill, near Leatherwood. The cemetery dates from the late sixth century or later. Bronze: length about 5.1 cm., width about 2.1 cm. Prongs bent far out of place. Elliston (1943), 39, and Fig. 1, No. 4; Meaney (1964), 242–243 (description of the cemetery with literature).

411.03 Guildford, Surrey Archaeological Society Museum (Fig. 14). Found in 1929 in the top soil of a Saxon cemetery of the sixth century in Guildown, Surrey. Bronze: length 5.1 cm., width 2.3 cm. Elliston (1943), 39, and Fig. 1, No. 5; Meaney (1964), 241–242 (description of the cemetery with literature).

411.04 Maidstone, Kent, Museum and Art Gallery. From grave 18 of the sixth- to seventh-century Saxon cemetery at Sarre, Kent, excavated 1863. Bronze: length 5.3 cm., width 2.4 cm. One prong broken off above middle. Elliston (1943), 35, and Fig. 1, No. 3; Meaney (1964), 135–136 (description of the cemetery with literature).

411.05 Lost (disintegrated after excavation). Found in 1772 in the Anglo-Saxon cemetery (possibly of the eighth to tenth century) at Sibertswold, Kent, in the grave of an elderly woman (grave 103). Iron: 9 cm. x 2.5 cm. Elliston (1943), 38, 39, and Fig. 2, No. 2; Faussett (1856), 119 (with figure); Hume (1863), 223–224, 226 (with figure); Meaney (1964), 136 (notes and literature on the graveyard).

411.06 Hollingbourne, Kent, collection of V. J. Newbury (in 1956). Found by Mr. Newbury in 1956 on the surface of a field at Egerton, Kent. Wrought iron: 6.3 x 3.5 cm. Similar to No. 411.11. Grove (1956), 269.

411.07 Hollingbourne, Kent, collection of V. J. Newbury (in 1947). Found about 1941 on the surface of a field between Egerton and Charing, Kent. Bronze: original length about 6 cm., width 2.9 cm. One prong broken off; the other broken off in the middle. Elliston (1947), 108, and Fig., No. 1.

411.08 Hollingbourne, Kent, collection of V. J. Newbury (in 1947). Found on the surface at Egerton, Kent. Brass or bronze: 6.4 x 3.5 cm. The bow is of a rounded rectangular shape. Elliston (1947), 108, and Fig., No. 2.

411.09 Maidstone, Kent, Museum and Art Gallery. Found 1939 by E. S. Jenkins in his garden at Otford, Kent. Bronze: 6.3 x 2.7 cm. Similar to No. 411.10. Another Jew's harp, found at the same time and place in bad condition, was subsequently lost. Grove (1956), 270.

411.10 Location unknown. Found 1955 about 120 cm. under the surface at East Sutton near Maidstone, Kent. Bronze: 7.4 x about 3.2 cm. Grove (1955), 210–212, including Fig. 3.

411.11 Otford, Kent, collection of R. D. Clarke (in 1955). Found in Mr. Clarke's garden, which "produces antiquities of all dates from prehistoric times onwards." Wrought iron: 6.7 x 3.2 cm. A fragment of the tongue still present. Grove (1955), 212, and Fig. 5.

411.12 Shooters Hill, London, collection of Frank C. Elliston-Erwood (in 1943). Found before about 1925, probably in the vicinity of Shooters Hill. Bronze: 5.5 x 2.4 cm. Elliston (1943), 34–35, and Fig. 1, No. 6.

411.13 Location unknown. Excavated before 1863 near Dove Point, Cheshire (near Liverpool). Bronze. Grove (1955), 212; Hume (1863), 223, 226, and Pl. XXII, No. 8.

411.14 Colchester, Essex, The Colchester and Essex Museum, 702.04. Bronze, 6.8 x 2.9 cm. Elliston (1943), 38–39, and Fig. 1, No. 1.

411.15 Colchester, The Colchester and Essex Museum, 3789.20. Found in Balkerne Lane, Colchester, "from a site where rubbish has been dumped ever since Roman times." Bronze: 5 x 2.4 cm. Elliston (1943), 38–39, and Fig. 1, No. 2.

411.16 Colchester, The Colchester and Essex Museum, 5282.26 (reported lost in 1943). Bronze. Elliston (1943), 39.

411.17 Oxford, Pitt Rivers Museum, Balfour No. 515. Purchased by Mr. Balfour from G. F. Lawrence in 1909. Excavated in Wood Street, Cheapside, London, E.C., at a depth of about 5.5 or 6 meters. Bronze: 5.2 cm. long, 2.8 cm. wide. Very possibly Roman, but also possibly later.

411.18 Rouen, Musée des Antiquités. Found in July 1861 in the foundations of a very large house at the corner of rue de la Grosse-Horloge and place du Vieux-Marché, once the route of the Roman road to Lillebonne. Gallo-Roman. Bronze: 8.3 cm. long, 2.4 cm. wide. Large end in the shape of a small oval.

411.19 Rouen, Musée des Antiquités. Found in June 1863 in Rouen, rue de l'Hôtel de Ville. Gallo-Roman. Bronze: 5.1 cm. long, 2.4 cm. wide. Fragments of the tongue are preserved.

411.20 Rouen, Musée des Antiquités. Found in February 1865 in the ruins of the large hypocaust chamber of a large house at the southwest corner of rue Rollon and rue de l'Impératrice. Gallo-Roman. Bronze: 4.8 cm. long, 2.5 cm. wide.

411.21 Rouen, Musée des Antiquités. Provenance unknown, but probably from Rouen, and probably Gallo-Roman. Very close in size and shape to No. 411.18. Bronze: 8.2 cm. long, 2.5 cm. wide. Large end in the shape of a small oval.

411.22 Château de Charon, par Neuvy-St.-Sépulchre (Indre), collection of Joseph Pierre (in 1935). A cast of it was made about January 20, 1896, by the Musée des Antiquités Nationales, Saint-Germain-en-Laye (Yvelines), for its collection. Dug up about 1895 in Levroux (Indre), with a Sequanian coin from near the time of the Roman conquest. Bronze: 5.5 x 3.5 cm. Pierre (1935–36), with fig., p. 104.

411.23 Location unknown. Found in 1839 near Issoudun (Indre) in a "kuba gauloise" of the sort called "margelle" by the people of Berry. Iron. Pierquin (1840); Pierre (1935–36), 7–11.

411.24–28 Nijmegen, Museum Kam, 75a (a group of bronze objects, including these five Jew's harps). There are no data on the source, but it is very likely that they are from Roman-period (first to fourth century) graves in Nijmegen and vicinity. Bronze: respectively 4.6 x 2.5; 4.7 x 2.2; 5 x 2.3; 4.8 x 2.4; 4.5 x 2.3 cm.; the last lacking one prong.

411.29 Excavated in the old Russian town site of Yekimauts, Moldavia (on the west side of the Dniester). Ninth or tenth century. Wrought iron: 5.2 x 3.1 cm. One prong broken off 1 cm. from the end of the other; about .4 cm. of the tongue still projects from the frame. Artsikhovsky, Vol. 65 (1959), 117 (with variant data on the find); Fedorov (1954), 18, and Fig. 7, No. 1.

411.30 Moscow, Institute of Archaeology of the Academy of Sciences of the USSR. Excavated at Novgorod. From the twelfth century. Iron. Kolchin (1964), 18–19 (mention).

411.31 Moscow, Institute of Archaeology of the Academy of Sciences of the USSR, Novgorod inventory No. 1–6–78. Excavated at Novgorod, in a level dating from 1462 and later. Iron: 6.4 x 3.2 cm. A little of the tongue still projects from the frame. Artsikhovsky, Vol. 65 (1959), 117, and Fig. 103; Kolchin (1964), 18–19 (mention); Thompson (1967), 76 (with photo), 101.

411.32–34 Location unknown. Excavated in 1849 in the ruins of Tannenberg Castle, near Darmstadt. The castle was built about 1200 and destroyed in 1399, so the three Jew's harps presumably date from the intervening time. Presumably bronze. The one illustrated in Hefner (1850) is 5.9 x 2.5 cm., and has about .8 cm. of the tongue left. Hefner (1850), 91, and Pl. VIII, Q; Klier (1956), 71, and Fig. 61.

411.35 Stendal, Altmärkisches Museum, 406/57–IV/24. Found in

Stendal. Bronze: 3.4 cm. long, 1.8 cm. wide. Richter (1957), with three photos.

411.36 Excavated at Vestergade, Kolding, Denmark. Iron. The frame is evidently well preserved, as is nearly half the main length of the tongue. The large end is of a distinctive triangular shape, like some Swedish examples. Skov (1957), with photo.

411.37 Location unknown. Found shortly before 1643 in a burial urn near "Hollojen," territory of Mandal, Norway (the island of Hille, or Hillöy, is probably meant). The cremation burial suggests a date before about A.D. 1000. "Copper, most brilliantly gilt" (presumably meaning gilt bronze). Elliston (1943), 38, 39; Worm (1643), 48.

411.38 Lund, Kulturhistoriska Museet, 5961. Excavated in Lund in 1890. Iron; medieval(?). Kjellberg (1948), 25, photo bottom row right; Rydbeck (1968), 258, 261, and Fig. 9, left of top right row.

411.39 Lund, Kulturhistoriska Museet, 12045. Iron; excavated in Lund; medieval(?). Kjellberg (1948), 25, photo bottom row left.

411.40 Lund, Kulturhistoriska Museet, 20310, x.c.4. Excavated in Lund, in the Apotekaren quarter, No. 5, on the property of the Skandinavska banken. Iron: 9 cm. long; from a layer of the fourteenth century. Rydbeck (1968), 258, 261, and Fig. 9, second from left.

411.41 Lund, Kulturhistoriska Museet, 21158. Excavated in Gyllenroks allé, Lund. Bronze; medieval(?). Kjellberg (1948), 25, photo bottom row center; Rydbeck (1968), 258, 261, and Fig. 9, lower right.

411.42 Lund, Kulturhistoriska Museet, 22792 c. Excavated in the St. Laurentius quarter, No. 1, Lund. Iron; medieval(?). Rydbeck (1968), 258, 261, and Fig. 9, left of lower right row.

411.43 Lund, Kulturhistoriska Museet, 26230. Excavated in the Altona Quarter, No. 7, Lund. Iron; medieval(?). Rydbeck (1968), 258, 261, and Fig. 9, upper right.

411.44 Lund, Kulturhistoriska Museet, 35371. Excavated in the St. Botulf Quarter, No. 2, Lund. Iron; medieval(?). Rydbeck (1968), 258, 261, and Fig. 9, middle of top right row.

411.45 Lund, Kulturhistoriska Museet, 38407:15. Excavated in Helgonabacken, in the center of Lund. Iron; medieval(?). Rydbeck (1968), 258, 261, and Fig. 9 left.

411.46 Lund, Kulturhistoriska Museet, no number. Excavated in Lund. Iron; medieval(?). Rydbeck (1968), 258, 261, and Fig. 9, middle of lower right row.

411.47 Lund, Lunds Universitets Historiska Museum, 17300. Excavated 1907–10 in the castle of the Danish governor at Skanör, Scania, Sweden. A fourteenth-century date is most likely; a date from the mid-thirteenth to the mid-fifteenth century is possible. Iron: 6.8 cm. long, 2.0 cm. wide. The holding end is unusually long and flat; about a third of the

23

tongue is preserved. Rydbeck (1935), esp. 40–41, 49, 58, and Fig. 109, No. 12; Rydbeck (1968), 254, 261.

411.48 Lund, Lunds Universitets Historiska Museum, 17300. Provenance and date as No. 411.47. Iron: 5.8 cm. long, 2.9 cm. wide. The instrument is quite rusted; the tongue appears to be preserved for its full length. Rydbeck (1935), passim, and Fig. 109, No. 13; Rydbeck (1968), 254, 261.

411.49 Lund, Lunds Universitets Historiska Museum, 17300. Provenance and date as No. 411.47. Iron: 5.9 cm. long, 3.2 cm. wide. The tongue is preserved for nearly half its length. Rydbeck (1935), passim, and Fig. 109, No. 14; Rydbeck (1968), 254, 261.

411.50 Lund, Lunds Universitets Historiska Museum, 17300. Provenance and date as No. 411.47. Bronze: 4.3 cm. long, 2.1 cm. wide. Both arms broken off. Rydbeck (1935), passim, and Fig. 109, No. 15; Rydbeck (1968), 254, 261.

411.51 Sigtuna, Sweden, Sigtuna fornhem, 66 1. Excavated in the center of Sigtuna, at Stora Gatan, in the Koppardosan quarter. Iron; medieval or later. Rydbeck (1968), 257, 261, and Fig. 8 right.

411.52 Sigtuna, Sigtuna fornhem, 1866:147. Excavated at the Dominican monastery at Sigtuna. Iron; from any time from the thirteenth to the sixteenth century. Rydbeck (1968), 257, 261, and Fig. 8 left.

411.53–56 Stockholm, Statens Historiska Museum, 17033:1459, 17237:1104, 17555:313, 19675:798. Excavated in the ruins of the Cistercian monastery at Alvastra, Östergötland, Sweden. Iron; three frames intact, one fragmentary. One perhaps from the fifteenth century; the others from any time from the twelfth century to recent. Rydbeck (1968), 256, 261, and Fig. 5 (photo of three of them).

411.57–59 Stockholm, Statens Historiska Museum, 21172:70–72. Excavated by the ruins of the Brigittine convent at Vadstena, Sweden (founded in 1371). Iron; the frames preserved essentially intact. Fifteenth century or later. Rydbeck (1968), 256–257, 261, and Fig. 6.

411.60–66 Stockholm, Statens Historiska Museum, 21174. Excavated in the ruins of Lindholmen Castle, Svedala, Scania, Sweden. Iron; one still has half its tongue; one lacks half an arm; one lacks arms entirely. Probably from the fourteenth to sixteenth century. Rydbeck (1968), 254–255, 261, and Fig. 3.

411.67 Stockholm, Statens Historiska Museum, 21174:171. Excavated at the Cistercian monastery at Vreta, Östergötland, Sweden. Iron; probably from any time between ca. 1200 to 1600. Rydbeck (1968), 257, 261, and Fig. 7.

411.68–70 Stockholm, Statens Historiska Museum, 23174, 27194, 27195. Excavated in the ruins of Falsterbohus Castle, Sweden. Iron; the tongue of one is preserved for the full length of the frame. Fourteenth century, or possibly fifteenth or early sixteenth. Rydbeck (1968), 254, 261, and Fig. 2 (text and photo indicate two instruments, but the note gives three inventory numbers).

411.71   Stockholm, Statens Historiska Museum. Excavated in the ruins of the late medieval convent in Ramundeboda, Laxå, Närke Province, Sweden.

411.72   Stockholm, Statens Historiska Museum. From Dalaborg, Bolstad Parish, Dalsland Province, Sweden.

411.73–79   Växjö, Smålands Museum, M. 17001. Excavated in 1930 in the ruins of Kronoberg Castle, Småland, Sweden. Iron, in various fragmentary states. Probably from the fourteenth and fifteenth centuries. Rydbeck (1968), 255–256, 261, and Fig. 4 (photo of five of them).

412. BULL-ROARERS

I know of no medieval objects identified as bull-roarers, and have not made any consistent search for them. It is, however, a type of instrument likely to have existed and survived. Until several possible specimens have turned up, establishing a series, one can not be certain that such an object as that listed below is actually a bull-roarer.

412.1   Dokkum (Frisia), Oudheidkamer. From a terp. Bone: 5.6 cm. long. Inscribed with apparently meaningless runes *dhlmo?*. Roes (1963), 82, and Pl. L, No. 13.

4211. BONE WHISTLES

The very numerous excavated bone duct flutes could be assigned to many types, according to such features as kind of bone, number of holes, presence or absence of a thumb hole, decoration, and shaping of the bone. For the present, however, I will simply distinguish the whistles from the flutes, as instruments without and with finger holes, respectively, and divide the whistles into the normal ones and the special "Frisian" types.

All these instruments were made from bones of mostly domestic animals and of birds, as far as they have been identified. The favored bone is the tibia, but some ulnae are also used, particularly those of large birds, such as the crane and stork. The most popular bone by far is the sheep's tibia.

In most cases the shape of the blowhole leaves no doubt that the instruments of types 4211–4213 were duct flutes. A few of the instruments have blowholes that were roughly round, showing no special edge on the bottom, and there is some possibility that these are cross flutes.

The typical example of type 4211 is simply a bone whose ends are cut off, so that what remains is a nearly cylindrical tube. Most show no other working but the blowhole. These are likely to be homemade instruments, rather than the products of skilled craftsmen. Some show quite crude hacking at the blowholes. These are signal rather than musical instruments, allowing only one tone, except by overblowing or stopping the lower end. Some may have been bird lures.

Except as otherwise noted, all the bone whistles and flutes in the Fries Museum and the Groninger Museum are from terpen in Frisia and Groningen provinces, respectively.

4211.01   Leeuwarden, Fries Museum, 20A–146. Found before 1900 at Jelsum, Leeuwarderadeel, Frisia. Length 11.5 cm. Broken off at bottom end, no finger holes present.

4211.02   Leeuwarden, Fries Museum, 24B–36 (Fig. 15). Found in 1903 at Finkum, Leeuwarderadeel. Length 8.9 cm. A notch below the blowhole is presumably for attaching a suspension cord.

4211.03   Leeuwarden, Fries Museum, 33–63. Found before 1900 at Aalsum, Oostdongeradeel. Length 9.1 cm.

4211.04   Leeuwarden, Fries Museum, 136–5. Found in 1913 at Westerlittens, Hennaarderadeel. Length 9.3 cm.

4211.05   Leeuwarden, Fries Museum, 201–99. Found in 1936 at Hempens, Leeuwarden. Length 9.4 cm.

4211.06   Found in 1936 at Bungay Castle, Suffolk. Dated in the twelfth or thirteenth century; other details unknown; perhaps more than one whistle. Braun (1936), 334; Megaw (1960), 11.

4211.07   Found in Rayleigh Castle, Essex. Dated in the twelfth or thirteenth century. A bird bone: 8 cm. long. Francis (1913), 171, and Fig. 5, No. 5; Megaw (1960), 11.

4211.08   Bydgoszcz, Poland, Muzeum im. Leona Wyczółkowskiego, 302 (deposited in the Museum für Vor- und Frühgeschichte, Berlin, in 1939). Found in the nineteenth century in Nicpon, near Fordon, Bydgoszcz District. Kamiński (1968), 14, with Fig. XI; Wieczorowski (1939), 351, and Pl. LXVI, No. 10.

4211.09   Poznań, Muzeum Archeologiczne, 1921:321. Found in Kępno, Kępno District. From the ninth century. Length 10 cm. Kamiński (1968), 14; Wieczorowski (1939), 350, and Pl. LXVI, No. 5.

4211.10   Poznań, Muzeum Archeologiczne, 1929:69–72. Found in an early historical settlement at Strzeszynek, Poznań District. A whole animal bone, intact and closed at the ends, 6.5 cm. long. A blowhole cut in the side near the middle; produces a loud, penetrating sound. Wieczorowski (1939), 351, and Pl. LXVI, No. 7.

4211.11   Poznań, Muzeum Archeologiczne, 1937:1390. Found in Gniezno in a layer dating from the end of the eighth and the beginning of the ninth century. Length 8 cm., diameter 1 cm. No finger holes; possibly broken off at what was the top finger hole. Kamiński (1968), 14, with Fig. XIV; Wieczorowski (1939), 350, and Pl. LXVI, No. 3.

4211.12   Poznań, Muzeum Archeologiczne, 38:1374. Found in the old Slavic town of Biskupin, Żnin District. Length 3.3 cm., diameter .8 cm.

According to Wieczorowski, from the seventh to the eleventh century; the town of Biskupin was occupied from ca. 700–500 B.C., but the whistle is from a later stratum. Kamiński (1968), 14; Wieczorowski (1939), 349, 354, and Pl. LXVI, No. 4.

4211.13   Poznań, Muzeum Archeologiczne. Excavated in 1938 in Ostrów Tumski, Poznań District. Length 4.5 cm. From the late eleventh or early twelfth century. Kamiński (1968), 14, with Fig. XII; Wieczorowski (1939), 351, 354–355, and Pl. LXVI, No. 6.

4211.14   Excavated at Bródno Stare, Warsaw District. Length 5.4 cm., diameter 1.5 cm. Two blowholes side-by-side at an equal distance from the top end. From the end of the eleventh century. Kamiński (1963), 555–556; Kamiński (1968), 14, with Fig. XIII; Kiersnowska (1951).

4211.15–16   Lund, Kulturhistoriska Museet. Two bone whistles, of unreported origin.

4211.17   Lund, Lunds Universitets Historiska Museum. Excavated 1907–10 in the castle of the Danish governor at Skanör, Scania, Sweden. A fourteenth-century date is most likely; any date from the mid-thirteenth to the mid-fifteenth century is possible. Tibia of sheep(?): 15.1 cm. long. Evidently only one small hole, near the middle; possibly not a whistle. Rydbeck (1935), Fig. 109, No. 1.

4211.18   Lund, Lunds Universitets Historiska Museum. Provenance and date as No. 4211.17. A bird bone: 8.9 cm. long; possibly intact. Rydbeck (1935), Fig. 109, No. 9.

4211.19   Stockholm, Statens Historiska Museum. Excavated in Lummelunda Parish, Gotland. Eleventh century.

4211.20   Stockholm, Statens Historiska Museum. Excavated at the ruins of the Cistercian monastery at Alvastra, Östergötland, Sweden. The monastery was occupied from 1143 to ca. 1530.

4211.21   Oslo, Historisk Museum. Excavated in Oslo. Probably from the thirteenth century. Length 4.1 cm.; evidently a notch near the lower end for attachment of a suspension cord. Sevåg (1969), 77, and photo Fig. 9, right.

4211.22   Oslo, Historisk Museum. Excavated in Oslo. Probably from the thirteenth century. Length 5.8 cm. Sevåg (1969), 77, and photo Fig. 9, left.

4211.23   Stavanger, Stavanger Museum. Excavated in Kvalbein, Ogna, Rogaland, on the south coast of Norway. Probably from a woman's grave of the ninth century. A bird bone: 5.4 cm. long; the blowhole is near the middle of the pipe. Sevåg (1969), 76, and photo and drawings Fig. 5.

4212. BONE WHISTLES, "Frisian" Types

Fourteen whistles from the Netherlands differ basically in form from the normal bone whistles. They are made from one side of a heavy bone, and worked into shape, in contrast to the standard use of the natural cylindrical shape of the bone. These whistles are the product of craftsmen, unlike those of the previous category. Numbers 01–11 are roughly rectangular or round in cross section at the blowing end, and gradually flatten out to a wider, thin cross section at the opposite end. The complete examples are pierced, about in the middle of the whistle's length, with a hole from side to side (considering the blowhole surface as the top); on each side of this hole is another pierced from top to bottom. The examples are related in decoration, with various combinations of incised lines and circles, and decorative piercings. The uniform, eccentric features of this type of whistle suggest that it had some special function. Perhaps the middle holes were fitted to pivots, or attached to the end of a string, from which the whistle was whirled around in a circle. As No. 11 is probably from the eighth or ninth century, it provides a rough date for the type.

Numbers 12–14 are of a different type. The mouthpiece end of these shorter whistles is flat, and the opposite end is of circular cross section, decorated with lines and depressions turned on a lathe (suggesting a later date).

4212.01 Leeuwarden, Fries Museum, 16D–40. Found before 1900 at Teerns, Leeuwarden. Length 11.4 cm. The fipple is preserved, and the whistle is playable. Roes (1963), 60, and Pl. IL, No. 6; Roes (1965), Fig. 33.

4212.02 Leeuwarden, Fries Museum, 18–38. Found in 1900 at Lekkum, Leeuwarden. Length 11.3 cm. Roes (1963), Pl. IL, No. 5.

4212.03 Leeuwarden, Fries Museum, 34B–58 (34A–58(?)). Found before 1900 at Wetzens, Oostdongeradeel. Length 7.2 cm.; the whistle part broken off. Roes (1963), Pl. IL, No. 9.

4212.04 Leeuwarden, Fries Museum, 34D–40 (Fig. 16). Found in 1908 at Jouswier, Oostdongeradeel. Length 11.0 cm.; the fipple is preserved. Roes (1963), Pl. IL, No. 7.

4212.05 Leeuwarden, Fries Museum, 153–18. Found in 1918 at Idsegahuizen, Wonseradeel. Length 9.5 cm. Not definitely a whistle, but resembles the mouthpiece end of one, the flat part broken off.

4212.06 Leeuwarden, Fries Museum, 1962–X–14. Found in 1962 in the town canal of Staveren, Staveren District, Frisia. Length 10.9 cm.; the fipple is preserved, and the whistle playable.

4212.07 Leeuwarden, Fries Museum, 1963–III–1. Found in 1963 in a castle-site at Metslawier, Oostdongeradeel, Frisia. Length 4.7 cm.; turned on a lathe; resembles the rest of Nos. 4212.01–11, except for lack of the portion opposite the mouthpiece, evidently broken off.

4212.08 Groningen, Groninger Museum voor Stad en Lande. About 8 cm. long; the mouthpiece end broken off.

4212.09 Dokkum, Frisia, Oudheidkamer. Roes (1963), Pl. IL, No. 4.

4212.10   Location unknown. Length 8.2 cm.; evidently broken off below blowhole. Roes (1963), Pl. IL, No. 8.

4212.11   Amersfoort, Museum Flehite. Excavated at Dorestad, and thus probably from the eighth or ninth century, when that town flourished. Length 8 cm.; most of the flat end broken off. Roes (1965), No. 191, pp. 57–58, and Pl. XXV.

4212.12   Leeuwarden, Fries Museum, 20–41. Found in 1909 at Cornjum, Leeuwarderadeel. Length 8.0 cm.

4212.13   Leeuwarden, Fries Museum, 20B–164. Found in 1905 at Britsum, Leeuwarderadeel. Length 7.9 cm.

4212.14   Leeuwarden, Fries Museum, 1961–IX–7. Found in 1961 in the village-center of Sexbierum, Staveren District, Frisia. Length 7.8 cm.

4213. BONE FLUTES

The flutes with finger holes are much more numerous than those without, and, perhaps only for that reason, are more widely distributed around Europe. They vary in number of finger holes from one to seven, and in execution from crude, homemade instruments to elegantly crafted ones. The majority are playable with one hand. Hardly any other generalizations are possible, except that, like the bone whistles, the flutes are seldom provided with reliable dates. Many of those listed here are likely older or newer than the Middle Ages.

Many flutes are in quite good condition, and would be playable if provided with fipples. (The few fipples preserved are of wood, as far as reported. The only other available material that might have been used for fipples, I believe, is beeswax. That beeswax was associated with bone flutes is made probable by Nos. 4211.14 and 4213.039, both of which have extra holes that could have been cut to improve on a defective instrument, whose original holes would then have been stopped up with wax.) The possibility of reconstructing their scales offers a particularly good subject for research; I hope that the beginnings made by Gerrit Vellekoop (1966), and by J. V. S. Megaw (1963) and others reported there and in Megaw (1968, "Problems"), 338–339, will be followed up by a broad study.

4213.001   Leeuwarden, Fries Museum, 15A–76. Found at Huizum, Leeuwarden, before 1900. From the sixth to eighth century. Bird bone: 21.6 cm. long. Four finger holes, one thumb hole. Boeles (1951), 202, and Pl. XXX, No. 17; Moeck (1954), 60; Moeck (1967), 28, 53, and Fig. 14.

4213.002   Fries Museum, 15A–139. Found about 1930 at Huizum, Leeuwarden. Length 18.6 cm. Two finger holes, one thumb hole. Roes (1963), Pl. XLVIII, Nos. 9–10; Vellekoop (1966), passim (including photos).

4213.003   Fries Museum, 20B–315. Found in 1906 at Britsum, Leeuwarderadeel. Length 15.5 cm. Five finger holes. Roes (1963), 60, and Pl. XLVIII, No. 8.

4213.004   Fries Museum, 21–53. Found before 1900 at Stiens, Leeuwarderadeel. Length 12.2 cm. The upper part is broken off at a finger hole; the preserved fragment has five finger holes, and a hole at the bottom of the back for suspension. Megaw (1968, "Problems"), 340.

4213.005   Fries Museum, 21A-289. Found before 1900 at Stiens, Leeuwarderadeel. Length 15.0 cm. Two finger holes.

4213.006   Fries Museum, 28–669. Found in 1905 at Hoogebeintum, Ferwerderadeel. Probably from before the ninth century. A bird bone: 23.1 cm. long. Four finger holes, one thumb hole. Boeles (1951), 202–203, and Pl. XXXI, No. 2; Moeck (1954), 60.

4213.007   Fries Museum, 28B–54. Found in 1905 at Blija, Ferwerderadeel. Length 18.6 cm. Three finger holes. The bottom end of the bone is intact and closed off, except for a small hole bored in it. Roes (1963), 60 (with Fig. 21), and Pl. XLVIII, No. 5.

4213.008   Fries Museum, 28B–85. Found in 1906 at Blija, Ferwerderadeel. Length 14.9 cm. Three finger holes.

4213.009   Fries Museum, 28B–190. Found in 1907 at Blija, Ferwerderadeel. Length 17.6 cm. Three finger holes.

4213.010   Fries Museum, 31–18. Found in 1917 at Hantum, Westdongeradeel. Length 8.6 cm. The lower end of a flute, broken off at the fourth hole from the bottom. Megaw (1968, "Problems"), 340.

4213.011   Fries Museum, 32–104. Found in 1930 at Hiaure, Westdongeradeel. Length 11.3 cm., maximum diameter 2.6 cm.; a short, fat flute similar to Nos. 4213.013 and 014. Decorated with many incised lines. Three finger holes, one thumb hole. Boeles (1951), 203, and Pl. XXXI, No. 3; Roes (1963), Pl. IL, No. 1; Vellekoop (1966), passim (including photos).

4213.012   Fries Museum, 34AA–38. Found in 1901 at Aalsum, Oostdongeradeel. Length 15.1 cm. Broken off below the first finger hole; traces of as many as three other finger holes remain.

4213.013   Fries Museum, 34B–42. Found before 1900 at Wetzens, Oostdongeradeel. Length 10.2 cm. Three finger holes, one thumb hole, and a suspension hole near the bottom of the back? Decorated with incised lines. Roes (1963), Pl. IL, No. 3; Vellekoop (1966), passim (with photos).

4213.014   Fries Museum, 34D–1. Found in 1906 at Jouswier, Oostdongeradeel. Length 12.8 cm. Three finger holes, one thumb hole. Decorated with incised lines. Boeles (1951), 203, and Pl. XXX, No. 16; Roes (1963), Pl. IL, No. 2; Vellekoop (1966), passim (with photos).

4213.015   Fries Museum, 50A–89. Found in 1907 at Deinum, Menaldumadeel. Length 16.1 cm. Four finger holes; a suspension hole near the bottom on back.

4213.016 Fries Museum, 65–12. Found before 1910 at Spannum, Hennaarderadeel. Length 9.0 cm. The lower end of a flute, including three finger holes. Decorated with incised lines.

4213.017 Fries Museum, 111–3. Found in 1909 at Hallum, Ferwerderadeel. Length 14.7 cm. Two normal finger holes, and another top hole near the blowhole.

4213.018 Fries Museum, 219–67. Found in 1934 at Wommels, Hennaarderadeel. Length 20.3 cm. Three finger holes. The top is broken off below the blowhole.

4213.019 Fries Museum, 1960–IX–17. Found in 1960 in the town center of Staveren, Staveren District, Frisia. Length 18.4 cm. Two finger holes.

4213.020 Fries Museum, 1964–IV–34. Found before 1940 at Oosterlittens, Baarderadeel. Length 8.5 cm. long. One finger hole. Incisions near lower end for attaching a suspending cord.

4213.021 Groningen, Groninger Museum voor Stad en Lande, 1877/VI 6. Found in 1877 at Saaxumhuizen, Baflo Parish. Tibia sinister of sheep: 11.2 cm. long. Three finger holes; on the back a suspension hole near the bottom. Folmer (1878), 193 (note); Pleyte (1877), 93, and Pl. XXIX, No. 3.

4213.022 Groninger Museum, 1884/I 82. Found at Warffum, Warffum Parish. Tibia sinister of sheep: 13.7 cm. long. Three finger holes; on the back a suspension hole near the bottom. Pleyte (1877), 96, and Pl. XXXIV, No. 12.

4213.023 Groninger Museum, 1884/I 83. Found at Warffum, Warffum Parish. Tibia dexter of sheep: 11.7 cm. long. Three finger holes, one thumb hole. Pleyte (1877), 96, and Pl. XXXIV, No. 13.

4213.024 Groninger Museum, 1887/VI 23. Found in the Hoogte Borgshof at Farmsum, Delfzijl Parish, Groningen. Tibia sinister of sheep: 13.6 cm. long. Four finger holes.

4213.025 Groninger Museum, 1890/VI 11. Found at Westerwijtwerd, Middelstum Parish. Ulna of swan: 21.1 cm. long. Four finger holes. Roes (1963), Pl. LVIII, No. 1.

4213.026 Groninger Museum, 1890/VI 12 (Fig. 17). Found in the terp north of Feerwerd, Ezinge Parish. Tibia dexter of sheep: 14.3 cm. long. Five finger holes; on the back a suspension hole near the bottom.

4213.027 Groninger Museum, 1891/VI 25. Found at Westerwijtwerd, Middelstum Parish. Tibia sinister of sheep: 14.5 cm. long. Three finger holes.

4213.028 Groninger Museum, 1891/VI 38. Found in 1891 at Valkum,

Winsum Parish. Metatarsus dexter of sheep: 11.6 cm. long. Four finger holes, but the top one appears to have been added recently.

4213.029 Groninger Museum, 1891/VI 39. Found at Schillingham, Winsum Parish. Tibia dexter of sheep: 16.6 cm. long. Three finger holes. Roes (1963), Pl. XLVIII, No. 6.

4213.030 Groninger Museum, 1894/VI 3. Found at Aduard, Aduard Parish. Tibia sinister of sheep: 13.0 cm. long. Three finger holes, one thumb hole; a small suspension hole near the bottom of the back. Megaw (1963), 87, and 93, note 10.

4213.031 Groninger Museum, 1917/VII 8. Found in the village terp east of the church at Jukwerd, Appingedam Parish. Tibia dexter of sheep: 13.2 cm. long. Three finger holes, thumb hole; at the bottom of the back a suspension hole. The wooden fipple, now lost, was still in place when the flute was found.

4213.032 Groninger Museum, 1920/II 148. Found between 1902 and 1914 in a cemetery in a terp at Aalsum, Oldehove Parish. Length 15.4 cm. Four finger holes, one thumb hole. Decorated with crude lines, and one circle-and-dot on the front.

4213.033 Groninger Museum, 1920/II 149. Found under the same circumstances as the above item. Length 16.2 cm. Three finger holes.

4213.034 Groninger Museum, 1921/I 13. Found in 1918 or 1919 in the terp north of the church at Rottum, Kantens Parish. Tibia of sheep: 11.9 cm. long. Three finger holes; the upper part of the blowhole is missing.

4213.035 Groninger Museum, 1921/I 28. Found in the terp west-northwest of the church at Westeremden, Stedum Parish. A bird bone: 10.7 cm. long. Two finger holes; but possibly broken off at a third.

4213.036 Groninger Museum, 1921/I 57. Found as the above item. A bird bone: 17.9 cm. long. Three finger holes.

4213.037 Groninger Museum, 1946/V 13 (1959/X 3). Found at Toornwerd. Tibia sinister of sheep or goat: 12.8 cm. long. Three finger holes, one thumb hole; a suspension hole on the back near the bottom end. Decorated with 23 circle-and-dot ornaments, mostly between the blowhole and the first finger hole.

4213.038 Groningen, Biologisch-Archeologisch Institut. Three finger holes; a suspension hole near the bottom front; the back not seen. Roes (1963), Pl. XLVIII, No. 7.

4213.039 Groningen, Biologisch-Archeologisch Institut. Six finger holes, arranged in two sets of three each, strongly suggesting that the flute was altered after manufacture by plugging up the first holes and boring a new set; the back not seen. Roes (1963), 60, and Pl. XLVIII, No. 4.

4213.040   Staveren(?), Frisia, private collection (in 1964). Found in the town center of Staveren, Staveren District.

4213.041   Leiden, Rijksmuseum van Oudheden, e 1953/8.1. Said to be from Elst. A bird bone: 19.5 cm. long. Four finger holes.

4213.042   Leiden, Rijksmuseum van Oudheden. Excavated at Dorestad, Utrecht Province, and probably dating from the eighth or ninth century, when the town flourished. A bird bone (tibia of swan?): 16.2 cm. long. Broken off at the top finger hole. Roes (1965), No. 192, p. 58, and Pl. XXV.

4213.043   Copenhagen, Nationalmuseet, 773/50. Found near the surface at Hals Skanse, Hals Parish, Kjær District, Aalborg County, Denmark. Length 15.5 cm. Broken off at both ends, but the essentials intact. Three finger holes, thumb hole. Nielsen (1951), 148, and Fig. 5.

4213.044   Copenhagen, Nationalmuseet, 838/50. Found in a sand layer under the floor of Egelund farm, Engesvang Parish, Hids District, Viborg County, Denmark. The farm was built in 1869, and thus the flute might be no older than this date. Tibia of sheep: 17.5 cm. long. Four finger holes; a suspension hole on the back near the bottom. The wooden fipple is preserved, held in place by two iron nails. Nielsen (1951), 148–149, 151, and Fig. 6.

4213.045   Copenhagen, Nationalmuseet, A 22140. Excavated at the site of a neolithic settlement at Hammeren, Bornholm Island, but probably really medieval or later. Tibia of sheep: 14.5 cm. long; broken off at blowhole. Five finger holes. Decorated with a number of shallow holes and cuts. Behn (1954), 4–5, and Pl. 1; Brøndsted (1960), III, 375 (photo), 443 (bibliography); Megaw (1963), 90, 91; Moeck (1954), 59, 61–62, and Fig. 5; Moeck (1967), 29, 54, and Fig. 21; Nielsen (1951), 147, 150–151, and Fig. 3; Skjerne (1931–39), 312.

4213.046   Copenhagen, Nationalmuseet, D 550. Tibia of sheep: 17.5 cm. long. Three finger holes. Nielsen (1951), 148, and Fig. 4.

4213.047   Svendborg, Denmark, Svendborg Amts Museum, 11995. Found in Svendborg, in a stratum with fragments of medieval pottery. Length 14 cm. Two finger holes. Nielsen (1951), 150, and Fig. 9.

4213.048   Odense, Denmark, Fyns Stiftsmuseum, B 2582. Found in a peat bog in Revsvindinge, Revsvindinge Parish, Vindinge District, Svendborg County. Length 15.6 cm. Four finger holes. Nielsen (1951), 149, and Fig. 8.

4213.049   Aalborg, Denmark, Historisk Museum, 8756. Found in Budolfi Square in Aalborg, in a stratum of A.D. 1000–1200. Length 15.2 cm. Two finger holes, one thumb hole. The mouthpiece has the beak shape of a recorder. Nielsen (1951), 149, and Fig. 7.

4213.050   Bergen, Hanseatiske Museum. Excavated in Bergen, under the Hanseatic Bridge. Leg bone of sheep or goat. Four finger holes; fipple preserved; playable. Sevåg (1969), 78, and Fig. 14b (i.e., third from left).

4213.051 Tromsö, Norway, Tromsö Museum. Found in a shipwreck at Træna, Nordland, Norway. Probably from the late Middle Ages. Bone of sheep or goat: 20 cm. long. Two finger holes, 1 thumb hole; fipple preserved; playable. Sevåg (1969), 78, and Fig. 14c (second from left).

4213.052 Tromsö, Tromsö Museum. Found near the same shipwreck as No. 4213.051. Probably late Middle Ages. Leg bone of sheep or goat: 13.3 cm. long. The top end with the blowhole is broken off. Two finger holes and a thumb hole opposite a point between them. Sevåg (1969), 78, and Fig. 14d (fourth from right).

4213.053–056 Lund, Kulturhistoriska Museet. Four intact flutes, possibly not medieval. One has 4 finger holes, one has 3, and two have 2.

4213.057 Lund, Lunds Universitets Historiska Museum. Excavated 1907–10 in the castle of the Danish governor at Skanör, Scania. Most likely fourteenth century, possible ca. 1250–1450. Tibia of sheep: 13.7 cm. long. Intact, with blowhole and 3 finger holes. Rydbeck (1935), Fig. 109, No. 2.

4213.058 Lund, Lunds Universitets Historiska Museum. Found and dated as No. 4213.057. Tibia of sheep(?): 26.9 cm. long. Intact, with blowhole and 3 finger holes. When found, the flute still had its wooden fipple, which has since disappeared. Rydbeck (1935), Fig. 109, No. 3a–b.

4213.059 Lund, Lunds Universitets Historiska Museum. Found and dated as No. 4213.057. Length 8.4 cm. Preserved: the top end, with the blowhole, a finger hole and the remains of another finger hole at the break. Rydbeck (1935), Fig. 109, No. 4.

4213.060 Lund, Lunds Universitets Historiska Museum. Found and dated as No. 4213.057. A fragment: 7.3 cm. long: the top end, with the blowhole. Rydbeck (1935), Fig. 109, No. 5.

4213.061 Lund, Lunds Universitets Historiska Museum. Found and dated as No. 4213.057. A fragment: 8.1 cm. long; the top end, with the blowhole. Rydbeck (1935), Fig. 109, No. 6.

4213.062 Lund, Lunds Universitets Historiska Museum. Found and dated as No. 4213.057. A bird bone(?): 12.8 cm. long. A fragment, broken at one end, with two holes on the front, neither one clearly a blowhole. Rydbeck (1935), Fig. 109, No. 8.

4213.063 Lund, Lunds Universitets Historiska Museum. Found and dated as No. 4213.057. A fragment: 8.9 cm. long (possibly the original length), with blowhole and 3 finger holes. Rydbeck (1935), Fig. 109, No. 10.

4213.064 Simrishamn, Sweden, Österläns Museum, 2024. From Österlän District, Scania. Fragment: with at least 3 finger holes. Moeck (1954), 63, and Fig. 10; Oldeberg (1950), 51.

4213.065 Stockholm, Musikhistoriska Museet. From Moravia. Foreleg of pig. Two finger holes (but broken off below the second one), one thumb hole. The hardwood fipple is preserved. Oldeberg (1950), 52–54, and Fig. 27.

4213.066 Stockholm, Nordiska Museet, 147 126. From Skansen near Kalmar, Småland; medieval. Blowhole, 3 finger holes. Moeck (1954), 64, and Fig. 14; Moeck (1967), 28, 53, and Fig. 11; Oldeberg (1950), 52, and Fig. 23.

4213.067 Stockholm, Statens Historiska Museum, 25 095:15. Excavated at the Cistercian monastery at Alvastra, Östergötland, Sweden, occupied from 1143 to ca. 1530. Tibia of sheep(?): 12.3 cm. long. Blowhole and 4 finger holes; broken off at the fourth hole.

4213.068 Stockholm, Statens Historiska Museum, 25 095:16. Excavated and dated as No. 4213.067. Tibia of sheep(?): 16.7 cm. long. Blowhole and 3 finger holes.

4213.069–080 Stockholm, Statens Historiska Museum. Twelve fragmentary bone flutes, excavated and dated as No. 4213.067.

4213.081 Stockholm, Statens Historiska Museum, 5208:1635. From the "Svarta Jorden," on the island of Birka (Björkö), Adelsö Parish, Uppland, in Lake Mälar. From the ninth or tenth century. Length 14.4 cm. Blowhole and 2 finger holes. Moeck (1954), 63–64, and Fig. 12; Moeck (1967), 27, 53, and Fig. 8; Oldeberg (1950), 51, and Fig. 21.

4213.082–084 Stockholm, Statens Historiska Museum. Excavated at Eketorp, Gräsgårds Parish, Öland. From ca. A.D. 1000–1250. Three incomplete flutes; one with both ends broken off, preserving 3 finger holes; another of the same description; a third with blowhole and 2 finger holes.

4213.085 Stockholm, Statens Historiska Museum. From Kalmar Old Town, Småland; medieval. Six finger holes, the first and sixth smaller, and one thumb hole. Broken off at the top, and lacking the blowhole. Moeck (1954), 62–63, and Fig. 6; Moeck (1967), 29, 54, and Fig. 22; Oldeberg (1950), 52, and Fig. 24.

4213.086 Stockholm, Statens Historiska Museum. From Kalmar Old Town. Intact, with blowhole and 3 finger holes.

4213.087 Stockholm, Statens Historiska Museum. Found at Levene gård, Levene Parish, Västergötland. A tibia, probably of a sheep. Blowhole and 3 finger holes, broken off at the third one. Moeck (1954), 63, and Fig. 11; Oldeberg (1950), 51–52, and Fig. 22.

4213.088 Stockholm, Statens Historiska Museum. Excavated at Lindholmen Castle, Svedala Parish, Scania. From the early fourteenth century or later. A fragment, with 3 finger holes.

4213.089 Stockholm, Statens Historiska Museum, 27 600:65+ R 8. Excavated in Lödöse, Västergötland. Dated between twelfth century and 1473. Tibia of sheep(?): 18.0 cm. long. Complete, with blowhole and 3 finger holes.

4213.090 Stockholm, Statens Historiska Museum. Excavated and dated as No. 4213.089. Broken off at both ends, with 2 finger holes on the remaining portion.

4213.091 Stockholm, Statens Historiska Museum. Excavated at Ragnhildsholmen Castle, Ytterby Parish, Bohuslän. Dated between 1256 and 1319. Blowhole and one finger hole.

4213.092–093 Stockholm, Statens Historiska Museum. Two fragmentary flutes, excavated at the Antonite monastery, Ramundeboda, dating from between the end of the fifteenth century and 1529. One with one finger hole, the other with three.

4213.094 Stockholm, Statens Historiska Museum. Excavated in Sigtuna, Uppland. Tibia of sheep; intact, with blowhole and 5 finger holes.

4213.095 Stockholm, Statens Historiska Museum. Excavated at the site of the State Archives, Stockholm. Intact, with blowhole and 3 finger holes.

4213.096 Stockholm, Statens Historiska Museum. Excavated at the Brigittine convent at Vadstena, and datable between the founding of the convent (1371) and 1595. Intact, with blowhole, 2 finger holes, 2 thumb holes.

4213.097 Stockholm, Statens Historiska Museum. Excavated at the Cistercian monastery at Varnhem; datable between 1150 and 1532. A fragment, including the blowhole.

4213.098 Stockholm, Statens Historiska Museum. Excavated at Veinge church, Halland. Tibia of sheep(?): 13.6 cm. long. Intact, except for fragments broken off at upper end; blowhole and 3 finger holes.

4213.099 Stockholm, Statens Historiska Museum. Excavated from a medieval dwelling at the Cistercian monastery at Vreta, Östergötland. Datable between 1162 and ca. 1600. Length 15.8 cm. Intact, with blowhole and 3 finger holes. Moeck (1954), 64, and Fig. 13; Oldeberg (1950), 52, and Fig. 26.

4213.100 Stockholm, Statens Historiska Museum. Excavated as No. 4213.099. Broken off at the blowhole; 4 finger holes, and a fifth not bored through. Moeck (1954), 63, and Fig. 8; Oldeberg (1950), 52, and Fig. 25.

4213.101 Stockholm, Statens Historiska Museum. Excavated at the Vreta monastery. A fragment, broken at the mouthpiece end, and preserving 3 finger holes.

4213.102 Berlin, Märkisches Museum (in 1876). Found in the vicinity of Nieder-Landin, Kreis Angermünde, Uckermark, near the Oder. Friedel (1876), 45.

4213.103–104 Berlin, Märkisches Museum (in 1939). Found together in Blankenberg, near Berlin. Wieczorowski (1939), 354.

4213.105 Eisenach, Wartburg-Museum. From near the Wartburg. Twelfth century. Length 9.4 cm. Three finger holes, thumb hole. Decorated with groups of dots on front and back. Moeck (1954), 60, 61, and Fig. 2; Moeck (1967), 33, 54, and Fig. 24; Sachs (1940), Pl. II, C.

4213.106 Excavated at Hedeby (medieval Haithabu), Schleswig-Holstein, Germany. Viking period (ninth-eleventh century). Tibia of goose or crane: 21.2 cm. long. Damaged at both ends; blowhole and three finger holes preserved. Jankuhn (1943), Fig. 79, p. 162; Megaw (1960), 11, and Figs. 1 and 3.

4213.107 Kassel, Landesmuseum. Excavated in 1953 in the old bed of the Ahna, in the Kassel Altstadt. From the "high Middle Ages." Three finger holes; back not seen. Niemeyer (1955, "Flöteninstrumente"), 334 (with drawing).

4213.108 Neubrandenburg (Mecklenburg), Verein . . . (in 1873). Found in 1872 in a peat bog near Neubrandenburg. Foreleg-bone of a small animal, perhaps a dog. Three finger holes, one thumb hole. A shallow indentation in the middle, perhaps for attaching a cord. Virchow (1873), 191–192 (with engravings).

4213.109 Stralsund, Provinzialmuseum (in 1876). Friedel (1876), 45.

4213.110 Found in Ostrów Lednicki, Gniezno District, Poland. Medieval. Some whistles also found there are not included in the present inventory. Wieczorowski (1939), 350, 354.

4213.111 Poznań, Muzeum Archeologiczne, 1901:558. Found in Kowalewo, Kościan District, Posen Province, Poland. From the early Middle Ages. Length 17.5 cm. Four finger holes, thumb hole. Richly decorated with circle-and-dot patterns. Kamiński (1963), 554; Kamiński (1968), 16, and Fig. XVI; Wieczorowski (1939), 350, 354, and Pl. LXVI, No. 9.

4213.112 Found in the excavation of an early settlement at Lubicz, Toruń District, Poland. From the seventh or eighth century. Fragment: 5.5 cm. long; only the top half is preserved, including the blowhole. Possibly not an instrument. Wieczorowski (1939), 350, and Pl. LXVI, No. 2.

4213.113 Międzyrzecz, Muzeum. From Międzyrzecz, Posen Province, Poland. From the early Middle Ages. Length 12.5 cm. Three finger holes, one thumb hole. Richly decorated with circles-and-dots. Feicht (1962), col. 1386; Kamiński (1963), 554; Kamiński (1968), 16, and Fig. XVII.

4213.114 From Kruszwica, Bydgoszcz Province, Poland. Early medieval. Feicht (1962), col. 1386; Kamiński (1968), 16.

4213.115 From Kruszwica, Bydgoszcz Province, Poland. Early medieval. Unfinished. Feicht (1962), col. 1386; Kamiński (1968), 16–17.

4213.116 Bucharest, collection of Viorel Cosma(?). Excavated in Garvan (Dinogetia), Romania, in 1960. Tenth century. A bird bone: 11.5 cm. long. Four finger holes; decorated with lines below the bottom finger hole. Broken off below the blowhole. Cosma (1966), 14, and Fig. 16; Mitrea (1962), with drawings and photos; Moeck (1967), 34.

4213.117 Excavated in 1954 in Garvan (Dinogetia), Romania. Tenth century. Fragment: 8.4 cm. long. Cosma (1966), 14; Mitrea (1962), 199.

4213.118 London, Institute of Archaeology of London University, CXX B III 5. Excavated in Rose Lane, Canterbury, in 1953. A bird bone: 18.7 cm. long, with 3 finger holes. From the twelfth or thirteenth century. Megaw (1968, "Earliest . . . Instruments"), 125; Megaw (1968, "End-Blown Flute"), with Pl. XXIII, C; Megaw (1968, "Palaeo-Organology"), 339.

4213.119 Found at Castle Hill, Folkestone, Kent. Twelfth or thirteenth century. A bird bone: 9.8 cm. long; the lower part broken off. Two finger holes, possibly more originally. Megaw (1960), 11; Pitt-Rivers (1883), 456, 464, and Pl. XX, No. 35.

4213.120 Excavated 1964 at Abbotsford House, Keynsham, Somerset (on the site of Keynsham Abbey). Probably from the fourteenth century, or not long before or after. Cannon-bone of fallow deer: 16.5 cm. long. Part missing at top, but knife-edge of blowhole preserved; 5 finger holes, 1 thumb hole. Barrett (1969), with drawings and a tablature.

4213.121 Excavated in 1930 at Lydney Castle, Gloucestershire. From the twelfth or thirteenth century. A bird bone: 5.2 cm. long. Broken off at top; two finger holes extant; broken in the middle of a third one. Casey (1931), 254, and Pl. XXXVI, No. 2; Megaw (1960), 11.

4213.122 Norwich, Castle Museum. Excavated in Calthorpe House, Norwich. From the eleventh or early twelfth century. Broken; 3 finger holes. Megaw (1968, "End-Blown Flute"), 149.

4213.123–124 Salisbury Museum. From Old Sarum; called "Roman" by the museum, but more likely medieval. Each has 3 finger holes. Megaw (1960), 11.

4213.125 Salisbury Museum. From Old Sarum; called "Roman" by the museum, but more likely medieval. Four finger holes. Megaw (1960), 11.

4213.126 Oxford, Ashmolean Museum(?). Excavated in 1939 in the medieval village of Seacourt, Berkshire. From the mid-twelfth to fourteenth century. Apparently a bird bone; fragment: 3.9 cm. long. Two finger holes preserved. Biddle (1961–62), 184, and Fig. 32, No. 5.

4213.127 Norwich, Castle Museum, 12.950 (1030). From the ninth-century level of a pit at Thetford, Norfolk. Leg bone of a crane: 19.5 cm. long; with blowhole and 3 finger holes. Megaw (1960), 10, 11, and Pl. II, No. 11; Megaw (1968, "End-Blown Flute"), 149, and Pl. XXIII, D.

4213.128 Norwich, Castle Museum. From Thorpe-next-Norwich. Saxon(?). Tibia of crane(?): broken. Megaw (1960), 11.

4213.129 Cardiff, National Museum of Wales, 32–429/12. Excavated at White Castle, Monmouthshire. Probably second half thirteenth century. Length 19 cm.; square cross section. Blowhole, 5 finger holes, 2 thumb holes, a small suspension hole on the back near the lower end.

Decorated with 235 dots. Harrison (1964), Fig. 52; Megaw (1961); Megaw (1963); Moeck (1967), 36, 54, and Fig. 31.

4213.130   York, Yorkshire Museum. Excavated in Clifford Street, York. Late Saxon. About 10 cm. long. Broken off at both ends, but the three preserved finger holes are the original number. Megaw (1960), 11; Waterman (1959), 91, and Fig. 19, No. 10.

4213.131   York, Yorkshire Museum. Excavated in Clifford Street, York. Late Saxon. About 19 cm. long. Broken off at both ends, but the three preserved finger holes are the original number. Megaw (1960), 11; Waterman (1959), 91, and Fig. 19, No. 11.

4221. ANTLER WHISTLES

A large number of objects made of antler tines, existing from the Bronze Age well into the Middle Ages, have often been identified as whistles. These artifacts (Fig. 18) are cut off flat at the wide end, and have a hole bored through the middle of the cut end, connecting to a notch on the inside curve of the antler, not far from the cut end. About in the middle of the inside curve there is a flat, shallow cut extending the full width of the antler (this cut is sometimes replaced by holes bored through the antler).

These objects do superficially resemble duct flutes, but I question that many, if any, of them were intended as instruments. The uniformity of their design suggests that all were made for the same purpose, but the middle cut seems so unnecessary for a whistle that some other use is strongly suggested. Roes (1963), 43–45, and Pl. XLI, gives good evidence that they were cheek pieces connecting the headstall and bit of a bridle, with the reins inserted through the hole, and fastened at the notch. It seems likely that only a whistle would require that the boring extend below the "lip" of the notch; boring only to the top of the notch would be conclusive evidence that the object was not a whistle. I have not been able to examine any specimens for this feature.

Wieczorowski (1939), esp. 349, 351–353, and Pl. LXVI, Nos. 1, 8, 11–13, reports on a number of mostly medieval examples of supposed antler whistles. Of these, Pl. LXVI, Nos. 8, 11 and 13 conform more or less to the standard type. No. 1 is a hollow object also proposed as a bagpipe mouthpiece, and No. 12 is worked differently, with the notch and hole on the outside curve of the antler.

I have not attempted to catalogue these doubtful objects.

4231. WOOD RECORDERS

4231.1   The Hague, Gemeentemuseum, 544045. Found under a fifteenth-century house at Dordrecht, and presumably as old as the house, or older. A single piece of elmwood, about 30 cm. long, turned on a lathe.

A *flûte à neuf trous;* "appears to have had metal or ivory rings at the ends." Harrison (1964), Fig. 69; Hunt (1962), 25; Moeck (1967), 35, 54, and Fig. 29.

4231.2 Excavated in a well in Würzburg. Datable between 1200 and 1300. Cherry wood: 9 cm. long. A fragment of the lower end: a suspension(?) hole near the end; above it, the double hole for the little finger, and two more finger holes. Moeck (1967), 35, 54, and Fig. 28.

4232. WOOD DOUBLE DUCT FLUTE

4232.1 Oxford, Library of All Souls College. Excavated at Christ Church, Oxford. From the late fifteenth or early sixteenth century. From one block of wood, about 31 cm. long; the left part about 20.3 cm. long. Each part has four finger holes and a thumb hole; the lowest notes of the right and left parts are *c″* and *g″* respectively. Bartha (1934), Pl. VI, No. 4; Galpin (1911), 147–148, and Pl. 35, No. 2; Megaw (1961), 179.

4233. WOOD TABOR PIPES

4233.1 Wrocław, Institut Historii Kultury Materialnej. Excavated in Opole, Poland. From the second half of the eleventh century. Elder wood; well preserved at the mouthpiece end, where it is carved into a thin beak, like a recorder's; the wood fipple is preserved. The instrument is split at the bottom, and the end is missing; the top finger hole seems to be indicated at the break; presumably there were two finger holes and a thumb hole near the bottom end. Now 26 cm. long. Feicht (1962), col. 1386, and Fig. 2; Hołubowicz (1958); Kamiński (1963), 554–555, with a drawing of a reconstruction; Kamiński (1968), 14–16, with Fig. XV (photo of reconstruction and original).

4233.2 Jaca, Alto Aragon, Spain, Brotherhood of St. Orosia. Bears the date 1402. Made of two halves, glued together and covered with snakeskin. Two finger holes and a thumb hole at the bottom. Moeck (1967), 41.

4234. WOOD DUCT FLUTES

These wooden instruments and fragments do not belong to any distinctive category of duct flutes.

4234.1 Moscow, Institute of Archaeology of the Academy of Sciences of the USSR, Novgorod inventory No. Il. 25–94. Excavated at Novgorod; from the end of the eleventh century. Softwood: 22.5 cm. long, 2.5 cm. in diameter, walls 3 mm. thick. Round cross section. Four finger holes. Damaged, but the essential parts preserved. Kolchin (1968), 88, and Pl. 84, No. 2 (photo).

4234.2 Moscow, Institute of Archaeology of the Academy of Sciences of the USSR, Novgorod inventory No. 5–8–1189. Excavated at Novgorod in a level dating from the years 1409–22. Softwood: 19 cm. long, 2.3 cm. in diameter, walls 3 mm. thick. Round cross section. Three finger holes.

The top end is damaged, but the knife edge is intact. Kolchin (1968), 88, and Pl. 84, No. 1 (photo).

4234.3   Stockholm, Statens Historiska Museum. Found in Slottsfjärden (the medieval harbor), Kalmar, Småland. Two finger holes, thumb hole.

4234.4–7   Wrocław, Instytut Historii Kultury Materialnej. Four wood fipples, dating from various times in the eleventh century, excavated in Opole, Poland. According to Kamiński (1963), 555, each is for a different flute type. Lengths respectively: 2.7, 4.8, 5.0, 3.0 cm.; diameters respectively: .8, 1.1, 1.2, 1.9 cm. Feicht (1962), col. 1386; Kamiński (1968), 17–18, with Fig. XVIII (two drawings of each).

4235. WOOD WHISTLE

4235.1   Wrocław, Instytut Historii Kultury Materialnej. Excavated at Opole; from the eleventh century. Cylindrical; ornamented with three slanting scratches; blowhole very near the top edge; no finger holes. Possibly not a whistle. Kamiński (1968), 13, and Fig. VIII.

4241. CERAMIC WHISTLES

Nos. 1-4, from Frisian terpen, are of a nearly identical pattern. A relatively narrow mouthpiece, containing the wind channel, widens out at the blowhole to form a small, enclosed resonance chamber. At the back, a little higher than the blowhole, the clay is pinched thin, and a suspension hole is pierced through.

Some ceramic whistles found in the Novgorod excavations have not yet been published.

4241.1   Leeuwarden, Fries Museum, 9–12. Found before 1900 in Staveren. From the mid-eighth to the eleventh century. Boeles believed it to be an import to Frisia. Length 6.1 cm. Boeles (1951), 450, and Fig. 78, No. 5.

4241.2   Leeuwarden, Fries Museum, 140–12 (Fig. 19). Found in 1915 near Franeker. Length 5.4 cm.

4241.3   Leeuwarden, Fries Museum, 171–13. Found in 1938 near Leeuwarden. Length 6.6 cm. Boeles (1951), 549.

4241.4   Workum, Frisia, private collection (in 1964). Found in 1962 at Workum.

4241.5   Excavated in Girvan, Romania. From the tenth century. Cosma (1966), 3 (mention).

4242. CERAMIC GLOBULAR FLUTE

4242.1   (Fig. 20) Excavated in 1963 in Novyĭ Saraĭ, Volgograd District, Russia. From the thirteenth or fourteenth century. Pear-shaped: 4.2 cm. long. Two finger holes, producing a fundamental scale of two whole-tone steps. Vaĭner (1965), with drawings.

4243. CERAMIC MULTIPLE DUCT FLUTES

Three instruments of a distinctive type come from a relatively small area of the lower Rhine. These duct-panpipes have a number of cylindrical holes bored from the top nearly to the bottom of the terra-cotta body. At the level of the top of these tubes, the body angles back at about 45 degrees, and a series of ducts is pierced in it, one for each tube. These ducts direct the air to the opposite (front) edges of the tube openings. Numbers 4243.1 and .2 are very close to each other in size and shape, although differing in the number of pipes. None were found under circumstances that allowed dating; they are probably all medieval, but the type may have originated in Roman times. Behn (1954), 111, reports a mold for the manufacture of ceramic panpipes found in the Roman pottery factory at Rheinzabern, Palatinate, without stating whether it is for duct panpipes of the present type.

4243.1   Excavated in 1887 or before in Velp, near Arnhem. The pottery style dates it in the ninth century or shortly before. Light gray pottery, with stripes of light green, blue, and yellow glaze: 16.5 cm. wide, 8.7 cm. high at one side, 6 cm. at the other. Eleven pipes, with pitches $f\sharp''$, g'', $g\sharp''$, a'', a'', $a\sharp''$, $a\sharp+''$, b'', c''', $c+'''$, $c\sharp'''$. Land (1894), 33–35; Salmen (1962), 278.

4243.2   Cologne, Niessen collection, No. 3231 (in 1913) (Fig. 21). White Lower-Rhine pipe clay; 16 cm. wide, 9.3 cm. high at one side, about 6 cm. at the other. Eight pipes, with pitches eb'', f'', $f\sharp''$, g'', $g\sharp''$, a'', bb'', c'''. Behn (1912–13), with photo and cross section; Behn (1954), 111; Salmen (1962), 278.

4243.3   Found in 1955 at the Esch in Gescher, near Coesfeld, Westphalia. Gray terra cotta with a green glaze on the top side of the mouthpiece surface. A hole for attachment of a suspension cord is broken off. About 9 cm. wide; evidently triangular cross section. Five pipes; the duct to the highest-pitched one is broken off; the other four have the pitches $db+''$, eb'', f'', g''. Salmen (1962), 277–279, with photo Fig. 2.

4251. METAL WHISTLES

On display in the Musée de Cluny, Paris, are twelve small metal whistles and two similar objects that may not be whistles. I presume the metal to be tin, although it could be bronze or lead. The museum's catalogue states that Nos. 1–8 of the list below were found in draggings of the Seine, and dates them in the fourteenth to fifteenth centuries.

4251.01   In the shape of a man's head, with the narrow, cylindrical mouthpiece projecting back from the lower end.

4251.02   Similar to 4251.01, but from a different mold.

4251.03   In the shape of a spear with attached banner with an inscription.

4251.04 Similar to 4251.03, but from a different mold. Photo Haucourt (1966), 67.

4251.05 (Fig. 22) In the shape of a signal horn, with suspension rings inside and outside the curve. About 6 cm. long.

4251.06 In the shape of a signal horn, with two suspension rings inside the curve, each attached to the end of a cord running through a third ring above the horn. About 3 cm. long. Photo Haucourt (1966), 67.

4251.07 In the shape of a drinking horn. About 2.5 cm. long.

4251.08 In the shape of a drinking horn with suspension ring. About 3 cm. long.

4251.09 In the shape of a fifteenth-century hand gun, with lettering. About 6 cm. long.

4251.10 In the shape of a cannon, with hexagonal barrel. About 5 cm. long.

4251.11 Cylindrical, decorated with feathers and wings, with a large suspension ring. About 3.5 cm. long.

4251.12 In the shape of a drinking horn. About 4.5 cm. long.

4251.13 With a four-vaned "windmill" in a Gothic arch, intended to turn in the stream of air. Perhaps not a whistle. About 5 cm. long.

4251.14 A "windmill" for an object like 4251.13.

431. BONE REEDPIPES

A small number of bone instruments have finger holes, but no blowhole, even though the upper part of the tube is intact. There is always a possibility that such an instrument is an unfinished duct flute, but I think the likelihood is very small. The practical procedure is to make the blowhole first, and then the finger holes, if the difficult job of voicing has succeeded. So it is quite safe to assume that these instruments are reedpipes. I hesitate to speculate on whether the reeds were single or double.

431.1 Leeuwarden, Fries Museum, 49A–153 (Fig. 23). Found in 1921 in a terp at Hatzum, Menaldumadeel, Frisia. A bird bone: 21.5 cm. long. Six equally-spaced finger holes. Megaw (1968, "Palaeo-Organology"), 343; Roes (1963), Pl. LVIII, No. 2.

431.2 Found near ancient Histria (modern Dobrudja region, Romania). From the fifth or sixth century. Material unknown, presumably bone: 16.5 cm. long. Four finger holes. Cosma (1965), 154.

431.3 Bulgarian, from the twelfth century. Six finger holes. Braschowanov (1952), col. 456 (photo).

431.4 Komárom, Hungary, Museum. Found in Ószony (Brigetio), Hungary. A bird bone, with squarish cross section; five finger holes. Possibly from a double pipe, but only the single bone is known. Palošija (1960), 66.

432. DOUBLE BONE REEDPIPES

Four instruments have been reported that consist of two bird-bone pipes held or joined side-by-side. In each case, the pipes have no blow-hole, and it is clear that the instruments were reed pipes. No mouthpieces are preserved, but they were surely of the single-reed type, as Bartha (1934) shows on the basis of the analogues. Some of the similar modern instruments have wind bags or horn bells, but is is impossible to say whether the excavated ones did.

All four instruments are from Avar Graves. (The Avars were a Ural-Altaic nomadic people who attacked and occupied parts of Europe in the sixth to eighth centuries.)

432.1 Budapest, Magyar Nemzeti Múzeum (Fig. 24). Excavated in 1933 in grave 49 of the Avar cemetery near Jánoshida, Szolnok District, Hungary. The cemetery dates from between A.D. 600 and 750. The pipe was found held in the hand of a male skeleton. The pipes are made of crane wing bones. Pipe A is 16.9 cm. long, and broken off at the lower end; pipe B is 17.5 cm. long. Pipe A has five finger holes, B has two. Traces of the bindings that joined the pipes show clearly. The workmanship is excellent. Bartha (1934) is a very thorough study, with photos of the pipes, a reconstruction and modern parallels. See also Baines (1960), 51–53 (with drawing); Megaw (1968, "Palaeo-Organology"), 345, and Fig. 76, No. 8; Niemeyer (1949–51) (with drawing); Palošija (1960), passim (with three photos).

432.2 Budapest, Magyar Nemzeti Múzeum. Excavated 1936–37 in grave 285 of the Avar necropolis at Alattyán (about four kilometers from Jánoshida), from the end of the seventh or the first half of the eighth century. The pipe was found at the right side of the head of the buried man. Two crane bones, 17.5 cm. long. The left one, essentially intact, has five equidistant finger holes. The middle of the right one is damaged, with only the bottom hole intact, but it appears that it might have had six holes, if there was one to match each of the five opposite, plus an apparent hole above the top one of the left pipe. Palošija (1960), passim, with photos Figs. 4a, 5a.

432.3 Budapest, Magyar Nemzeti Múzeum. Excavated as No. 432.2, from grave 477, with the same possible date. The pipe was found by the left upper arm of a young woman. Crane bones: 16 cm. long; both quite well preserved. There are five equally-spaced finger holes on each pipe, exactly opposite each other. Palošija (1960), passim, with photos Figs. 4b, 5b.

432.4 Zagreb, Arheološki muzej, 10499. Excavated in 1948 in grave 16 of an Avar-Slav necropolis at Bijelo Brdo, near Osijek (Croatia). From a man's grave of the second half of the seventh century. Ulnae of a large bird, both broken off roughly three-fifths of the way from the top; the lower ends are missing, and the lower part of what is preserved is damaged; both are now about 13 cm. long. The left tube preserves three holes, the right one two holes; there is no hole in the right tube opposite the top left hole, but the other holes are exactly opposite. Marković (1951); Palošija (1960), passim, with photo Fig. 1 and photo *in situ* Fig. 2.

433. WOOD SHAWMS

A Frisian shawm and an approximately coeval British one show a near identity that is a remarkable illustration of the close cultural relations of those regions in the Middle Ages. At the top is a short, slightly tapering tenon for attaching the mouthpiece. The main part of the pipe is cylindrical, but flattened on the front. The finger holes are in the middle of flat depressions; the spaces between these depressions are decorated with incised geometric designs, in part nearly identical in the two instruments. The bottom flares to form the familiar bell. The flaring is just enough to suggest that it is in imitation of the natural broadening of a bone pipe at the bottom. The principal differences in design are these: the Frisian pipe has a rudimentary pirouette just below the mouthpiece tenon, a thumb hole above the first finger hole, and a hole irregularly placed in the middle of the design below the lowest finger hole—perhaps a finger hole, but reminiscent of the vent holes on later medieval shawms. The Frisian instrument is more elegantly made than the British one. See the discussion of type 434 for speculations on the mouthpiece.

433.1 Leeuwarden, Fries Museum, 28B–209 (Fig. 25). Excavated in 1907 in a terp at Blija, Ferwerderadeel, Frisia. Probably dates from between about A.D. 750 and 1000. The present length of 24.3 cm. is probably very close to the original one. The front is split from the first to the fifth finger hole, and below that the instrument is badly damaged; most of the bell is missing, but enough remains to reconstruct the shape of the bell with confidence. Seven finger holes, the first six equally spaced 2.4 cm. from center to center, the last 1.4 cm. lower; thumb hole above first finger hole. The bore is about .5 cm. at the top, and may be estimated at .6 to .7 cm. for most of its length. The workmanship is of considerable quality. Boeles (1951), 203–204, and Pl. XXXI, No. 5; Megaw (1961), 179; Richardson (1959), 64.

433.2 York, Castle Museum(?). Excavated in Anglo-Danish (tenth or eleventh century) levels at the Hungate, York. Hawthorn or applewood. The two ends are preserved; a piece is missing in the middle. The top fragment is 7.8 cm. long and has three finger holes; the bottom fragment is 9.6 cm. long and has one finger hole. At least one more finger hole must have existed originally; assuming six finger holes, the original length would have been close to 21 cm. Megaw (1961), 179; Megaw (1968, "Palaeo-Organology"), 343, and Fig. 76, No. 5; Richardson (1959), 63, 64, 85, and Fig. 19, No. 20.

434. HORNPIPES

Three wooden objects from Frisian terpen offer something of a challenge as to interpreting their function. These are pipes about 12 cm. long, with square cross section, three equally-spaced finger holes, and a tapering tenon at each end. The pipes are completely symmetrical lengthwise, with no indication that either end has a different function from the other. The relationship of their design to that of type 433 is clear. The two types are essentially identical, except for the shorter length, fewer holes, and tenons at both ends of type 434. Even the decoration of No. 434.1 is almost an exact copy of that of 433.1.

Only one interpretation of these objects seems likely: they are hornpipes; at one end was attached a conical section of horn enclosing the reed, and at the other was attached the horn bell. This interpretation is confirmed by the striking similarity of the Frisian pipes to the wooden middle section of one of the eighteenth-century Welsh pibcorns in the Welsh Folk Museum, St. Fagans near Cardiff. This section is also symmetrical lengthwise, and is closely similar to the Frisian pipes in cross section and décor, but has six equally-spaced finger holes and a thumb hole (like No. 433.1). On the Welsh instrument, see Harrison (1964), Fig. 78; Megaw (1961), 178–179; Peate (1947), 21–22, and Pl. B, No. 8. The history and varieties of the hornpipe are well presented in Baines (1960), passim.

434.1   Leeuwarden, Fries Museum, 74C–231. From a terp at Achlum, Wonseradeel, Frisia. Boeles (1951) dates it ca. A.D. 750–1000, from the similarity of its design to that of No. 433.1. Length 11.7 cm., cross section 1.2 cm., bore averages about .5 cm. Finely decorated on front, back, and one side. Warped, and rather deteriorated. Boeles (1951), 203, and Pl. XXXI, No. 4.

434.2   Leeuwarden, Fries Museum, 77A–93 (Fig. 26). Found in 1912 in a terp at Wijnaldum, Barradeel, Frisia. Length 12 cm., cross section 1.2 cm. square, diameter of bore averages 6 mm. Unfinished *Kerbschnitt* patterns on the raised parts of the front are the only decoration. Nearly intact.

434.3   Leeuwarden, Fries Museum, 101Bis–1589. Found in 1925 in a terp at Ferwerd, Ferwerderadeel, Frisia. Length 12.3 cm., cross section averages 1.5 cm. on a side. Bore averages 7 mm. at one end, 6 mm. at the other. Marked only with a lightly incised "X" on one side. In fairly good condition.

435. BAGPIPES

The instruments listed here are not especially good evidence of the nature of the medieval bagpipe, all being of doubtful authenticity, and only one available for study.

435.1 Edinburgh, National Museum of Antiquities of Scotland (earlier in the possession of J. and R. Glen, Edinburgh). Scottish, carved with the initials R.McD. and the date 1409, but the authenticity of the date is in question. Chanter, and two drones an octave apart. Baines (1960), 115–116; Galpin (1911), 177–178; Hipkins (1888), 12; Langwill (1961–62), 66; van der Meer (1964), 139.

435.2 Kinlochmoidart, collection of N. Robertson M'Donald (in 1888; whereabouts now unknown). Said to have been played at the battle of Bannockburn (1314). One drone; the chanter has double little finger holes, like those of an old recorder. Hipkins (1888), 12.

435.3 Nürnberg, Germanisches Nationalmuseum (lost in World War II). Dated 1469, but the authenticity of the date is in doubt. Van der Meer (1964), 131.

441. CLASSIC OLIPHANTS

No other group of instruments has been preserved above ground in such numbers for as long as the oliphants. The special respect, and even reverence that has saved them is the natural response to the beauty of their material and workmanship and to their impressive dimensions, assisted by the familiar and effective press-agentry. The qualities that have preserved them have also led to extensive study of the oliphants by art historians. As a result, it is possible to be more certain about the time and place of their origin than with most medieval instruments.

To classify the oliphants, I have drawn a slightly arbitrary line between the "classic" oliphants and all later ivory horns. The classic oliphants are properly so called; they have a relative unity of style, and of time and place of origin; they are the instruments that the poets and their audiences understood by the name oliphant. They are much more numerous than the ivory horns of the latter Middle Ages, which are heterogeneous in material (walrus ivory alongside the classic elephant ivory), style, and origin.

Although a few earlier papers had been devoted to the oliphants (Bock, Cahier, Closson), the first careful, informed study was that of Otto von Falke (1929–30). Von Falke's work, in turn, has been superseded by the publications of Ernst Kühnel (1959; 1963 includes a good summary) and Hanns Swarzenski (1962). The convincingly supported conclusions of Kühnel and Swarzenski can be briefly summarzied; they should be understood as applying to all the oliphants of the present category, except for a few examples for which still more specific origins have been suggested. The oliphants were made by Islamic artisans working in Sicily or southern Italy (Apulia, Campania), in the cities of Bari, Palermo, Amalfi, and particularly Salerno. There is no evidence that any were actually made in Islamic lands, or in Byzantium. They were made strictly for the European market; Kühnel stresses that there is no evidence for their use in Islamic territories. It is unlikely that the oldest date from much before A.D. 1000. The eleventh century, perhaps the early twelfth, is the time when they were produced in quantity.

The classic oliphants, in shape, are simply elephant tusks hollowed out and cut off at each end to form a mouthpiece and bell. The one universal feature is a pair of smooth bands, recessed in the ivory several centimeters from each end, to each of which a metal strap was attached for attachment to a supporting chain. Normally, there is a narrow decorative band on each side of these suspension bands. Between the mouthpiece and the nearest suspension band, there is usually decoration to match that of the middle section, but sometimes the surface is smooth. The bell end is nearly always decorated with figures. Four main types of decoration can be distinguished. The commonest one has the middle zone covered with animals in a net of circles. The second has lengthwise facets between the suspension bands, filled with carvings. The third type has no decoration in the middle zone, except for a number of smooth, lengthwise facets. The fourth has scenes and figures of all sorts, particularly in circumferential bands. Holes in the surface of some oliphants show that they had been studded with ornaments of precious metal or gems.

It is a mistake to think of the oliphants as musical or even, in spite of the *chansons de geste,* signal instruments. Such precious and heavy horns were not carried to hunt or battle by anyone who cared about the horn or his own mobility. If they were blown at all, it was for ceremonial purposes. (Bragard, 1968, 59–60, states that "Quite a lot of oliphants have been recovered from the site of the battlefield at Agincourt, thus dating them from 1415." I have been able to verify only that in 1816, Sir Alexander Woodford, in command of occupation troops, oversaw the excavation of one of the three large common graves in which the noble French victims of the battle were buried, and from which he took a large quantity of armor and coins to England. If this excavation included horns or trumpets of any kind, the precise date that could be given them, and the fact that they were used in battle would make them very interesting objects for study.)

The buyers of oliphants were, of course, wealthy people. Their possession would have been limited to the nobility and the churches. Two functions are frequently documented, and may have been the main purposes for which the oliphants were manufactured. Many of them were kept by nobles, particularly in England, as symbols of their tenure of land, the land being granted (according to Scott (1814), I, lxviii–lxix) for the service of sounding a horn to warn of the approach of hostile parties. Some were held in the same British families until recently. Very many were acquired by churches in all parts of western and central Europe, where they often were used as reliquaries. Records as far back as the eleventh century show that there were once a very large number in churches (a thorough search of medieval church inventories would be a rewarding study). About half of the extant oliphants are still in churches, or were taken from them recently.

Comprehensive catalogues of the oliphants were planned as part of the study of Goldschmidt (1914–26), and by Ernst Kühnel. Although both scholars had done most of the work of gathering the material (Goldschmidt's photographic collection is in the Manuscript Room of McCormick Hall, Princeton University), neither lived to complete his work. The present list, being based largely on the published literature, rather than on a good collection of photographs, is strictly provisional. The literature contains many errors; many instruments have moved around. Since it is impossible always to be sure that instruments mentioned in different publications are identical, some may be listed twice in the present list, or, on the other hand, two might be identified as one. Some are probably omitted—no list published yet is near to being complete.

441.01   Aachen, Cathedral Treasury. Length 60 cm., bell diameter 13 cm. Weight 3 kg. Produces the notes b flat, b' flat, f''. Smooth mouthpiece end; middle decorated only with facets; bell end: steers and deer. The (later?) very rich carrying band has the repeated motto "dein eyn." Closson (1926), 284–285; Falke (1929–30), 516; Karstädt (1964), 32, and Pl. II; Kinsky (1929), p. 43, Fig. 1; Kühnel (1959), 36, and Fig. 1; Teichmann (1903).

441.01A   Aarau, Switzerland, Cantonal Antiquarium. An eighteenth-century ebony copy of 441.57.

441.02   Amsterdam, Rijksmuseum. Carvings in middle include Samson and the lion; bell frieze has hunters and animals. Falke (1929–30), 44.

441.03   Angers, Musée Archéologique St. Jean. Separate(?) mouthpiece, with rim protruding to sides. Mouthpiece end plain; in middle, about fifteen lengthwise facets; at bell, a frieze of men and animals. Cahier (1874), 40, 49–51 (with engravings; ascribed to Anjou); Falke (1929–30), 42; Kendrick (1937), 281; Molinier (1896, *Histoire*), 94; Swarzenski (1962), 41; photo *Enciclopedia universal ilustrada*, Vol. 39 (Barcelona: Espasa, n.d.), 1023.

441.04   Arles, Musée (formerly in St. Trophime, Arles). Middle undecorated. Buhle (1903), 102; Cahier (1874), 51–52; Kendrick (1937), 281.

441.05   Auch (Gers), Musée d'Art et d'Archéologie de la Ville d'Auch (formerly Auch, St. Orens Church). At mouthpiece and bell ends, frieze of animals in circles; in middle, seven or eight lengthwise bands with animals in circles and semicircles. Buhle (1903), 103; Kühnel (1959), 42, and Fig. 15; photo Tardy (1966), p. 222.

441.06   Baltimore, Walters Art Gallery (in 1925 for sale by a Berlin art dealer). Decorated with animals in a net of circles. Along entire inner curve, two entwined snakes. Falke (1929–30), 41, and Fig. 8 (erroneously ascribed to Metropolitan Museum); Kühnel (1959), 37, 41–42, 45, and Figs. 13–14.

441.07   Berlin, Museum Dahlem, K.3106 (formerly Berlin, Kaiser-Friedrich-Museum; obtained in 1838 for the Preussische Kunstkammer from the collection of Domherr von Warmbold, Heidelberg; believed to have come ultimately from the Speyer Cathedral). At mouthpiece and bell ends, frieze of animals in circles; in middle, animals in a net of circles. Falke (1929–30), 511, and Fig. 2; Kühnel (1959), 36–37, and Fig. 2; *Enciclopedia Italiana* 14 (1932), Pl. CLIII; photo Tardy (1966), p. 222.

441.08   Berlin, Kaiser-Friedrich-Museum (in 1930). Mouthpiece end plain; middle has three encircling bands with hunting scenes; at bell end, a wide band of stylized foliage. Traces of gilding remain; iron suspension bands. Falke (1929–30), 40–42, and Fig. 2; Swarzenski (1962), 31; Volbach (1923), 16, and Pl. 36.

441.09   Berlin, Kaiser-Friedrich-Museum (in 1929). Short, narrow European copy of the Islamic type. Falke (1929–30), 517, and Fig. 10; Kühnel (1959), 46.

441.10   Berlin, Zeughaus (lost in World War II). Close to 441.01 in design. Falke (1929–30), 516; Kühnel (1959), 36, 45, and Fig. 3 (detail).

441.11   Boston, Museum of Fine Arts, 50.3426 (formerly owned by the Counts of Waldersdorf; in 1928 for sale by J. Rosenbaum, Frankfurt a. M.). Length 53 cm., width at bell 13 cm. Decorated only with seven rather narrow circumferential bands of stylized foliage, four near mouthpiece end, three near bell end. Middle lightly faceted. Falke (1929–30), 42; Museum of Fine Arts, Boston, *Bulletin* 55 (1959), photo p. 96; Swarzenski (1962), with photo p. 29.

441.12   Boston, Museum of Fine Arts, 57.581 (formerly owned by the Counts of Eltz). Length 65 cm., greatest diameter at bell 13 cm. The small end is left closed, so that there never was any possibility of producing tones. Decorated with 21 panels in six encircling bands, with some real, but mostly mythological animals, and a man. The iron carrying chain is probably the original one. Swarzenski (1962), with photos on cover and pp. 32–33, 38–39.

441.13   Braunschweig, Landesmuseum, 107. Very close in design to 441.01. Gessler (1925), 90.

441.14   Braunschweig, Landesmuseum, 108. Falke (1929–30), 517; Gessler (1925), 90.

441.15   Braunschweig, Landesmuseum, 109. At ends, processions of animals; in middle, 14 lengthwise bands alternating animals with foliage. Falke (1929–30), 516, and Fig. 9; Kühnel (1959), 45, with Fig. 18.

441.16–17   Carlisle, Cathedral. Two damaged oliphants(?). Bridge (1905), 112–117; Maskell (1905), 241–242.

441.18   Cleveland, Cleveland Museum of Art (until about 1930 with the Guelf Treasure in the Braunschweig Cathedral Treasury). The "horn of St. Blasius." Length 49.5 cm., width 11.8 cm. at bell. Middle lightly faceted; at bell a frieze of animals. Falke (1929–30), 42; Kendrick (1937), 281; Milliken (1930), 168–169, and 2 pl., p. 174; Swarzenski (1962), 28, 40–41.

441.19   Copenhagen, Nationalmuseet (given to Ole Worm by King Frederick III in 1650). The undivided middle section is covered with circus scenes, fabulous beasts, hunters, warriors, animals; at bell end, a narrow procession of animals; the carrying bands are smooth, but not sunken. Length 50 cm. Falke (1929–30), 40–41, and Fig. 4; Skjerne (1931–39), 324, and Fig. 338; photo (detail) Tardy (1966), p. 140; Worsaae (1859), p. 158 (2 engravings).

441.20   Cracow, Muzeum Narodowe(?). Little carving. Bock (1860), 139, and Fig. 4 and 5; Buhle (1903), 103; Gessler (1925), 91.

441.21   Dresden, Waffensammlung (in 1929). Short, narrow European copy of the Islamic type. Falke (1929–30), 517; Kühnel (1959), 46.

441.22   Dublin, Holt collection (in 1959; in 1933 in coll. of Captain Plenderleith, London; said to have belonged to the Braithwaite family since 1640 or earlier). At mouthpiece, a procession of animals; in middle, animals in a net of circles; the bell end is cut off at the top of the outer decorative band next to the carrying band. Kühnel (1959), 37; Longhurst (1933), with photo.

441.23   Edinburgh, Royal Society of Antiquaries. Mouthpiece end plain; middle, animals in a net of circles; at bell, a procession of animals. Falke (1929–30), 514; Kühnel (1959), 37, 40; Maskell (1905), 243; Rice (1965, *Islamic Art*), Fig. 97; Waring (1858), Pl. 3.

441.24   Florence, Museo Nazionale. At each end, a frieze of animals in circles; in middle, 12 or 13 lengthwise bands with animals in processions. Falke (1929–30), 511, and Fig. 4; Kühnel (1959), 42–43, and Fig. 17.

441.25   Hanover, Kestner-Museum. In middle, animals in circles. Falke (1929–30), 514, and Fig. 7; Kühnel (1959), 37.

441.26   Hildesheim, Cathedral Treasury. Used as a reliquary. Buhle (1903), 103.

441.27   Jászberény, Hungary, Jász Múzeum (formerly in a church there). The "horn of Leelis (or Lehel)." Length 43 cm. partly broken off at the bell. Mouthpiece end plain; rather coarse chains of ornament surround the plain silver suspension bands; in middle, circus scenes with many jumbled animals and men; at bell end, animals in a frieze of entwined circles. Dalton (1914), passim; Falke (1929–30), 40–41, and Fig.

51

5; Gessler (1925), 91; Skjerne (1931–39), 323, and engraving p. 338; Thomas (1956), 398, and photo p. 399.

441.28   Klosterneuburg, Austria, Stift. Buhle (1903), 103.

441.29   Leningrad, Hermitage (formerly in Basilewski collection). Decorated with animals in a net of circles. Buhle (1903), 103; Falke (1929–30), 514, 516; Kühnel (1959), 37, 41.

441.30   Le Puy (Haute-Loire; formerly called Le Puy-en-Velay), Musée Crozatier. The so-called "horn of St. Hubert." At each end, an encircling band of animals; in middle, about eleven narrow lengthwise bands with stacked animals. With two metal suspension bands and chain. Kühnel (1959), 44, and Fig. 16; *Larousse de la musique* (Paris: Larousse, 1957), II, 125; photo Tardy (1966), p. 221.

441.31   London, British Museum. The "Clephane horn," long in the possession of the Clephane family, Carslogie Castle, Fifeshire; in the early twentieth century owned by the Marquess of Northampton. Length 57 cm., width 13 cm. at bell. Broken at the bell end; cracked, and a hole in the body. The undivided middle section is covered with scenes of quadriga racing, fighters on horseback, hunting, etc. Cahier (1874), 49–50 (ascribed to Northampton); Dalton (1914); Falke (1929–30), 40, and Fig. 3; Kühnel (1959), 37; Maskell (1905), 243; Scott (1814–17), II, 206–207, and pl. opp. p. 208.

441.31A   London, British Museum. A modern forgery, after 441.01 Kühnel (1959), 36.

441.32   London, Victoria and Albert Museum (formerly called the South Kensington Museum), 7953–1862 (acquired from the Soltikoff collection—No. 376 of the 1861 sale catalogue). (See Fig. 27.) Length 64 cm., diameter at bell 13.5 cm. A metal mouthpiece; above it, three animals in circles; in middle, animals in a net of circles; at bell end, a ring of animals in circles. Engel (1874), 227–228; Falke (1929–30), 511; Farmer (1966), 84, and Fig. 73; Goldschmidt (1914–26), III, 38 (with photo); Kühnel (1959), 37, 40, and Fig. 10; Kunz (1916), pl. opp. p. 63, No. II; Longhurst (1927–29), I, 50–51, and Pl. XXVII, top; Maskell (1905), 242, and Pl. LI.

441.33   Montmorency (Seine-et-Oise), collection of the Duke of Dino (in 1903; earlier Dijon, Baudot collection). Buhle (1903), 103; Molinier (1896, *Histoire*), 94.

441.34   Munich. The cut-off bell of an oliphant, converted to a baptismal water container (pyx). Was this also the fate of the other cut-off ends (Nos. 441.22, 39, 46, 51)? Goldschmidt (1914–26), IV, 68, 72; Swarzenski (1962), 28, 43.

441.35   New York, Metropolitan Museum (earlier Paris, Spitzer collection; before that in the Soltikoff collection). Decorated with animals in a net of circles. Buhle (1903), 103; Kühnel (1959), 37, 40, and Fig. 11; Kunz (1916), pl. opp. p. 63.

441.36 New York, Metropolitan Museum. Fragment; the upper half of an oliphant, cut in the middle, broken at the bell. Falke (1929–30), 511; Kühnel (1959), 37, 40, and Fig. 12.

441.36A New York, Metropolitan Museum. Considered a modern counterfeit after 441.41. Short and narrow; in middle, animals in a net of foliage. Falke (1929–30), 517; Kühnel (1959), 46. The Metropolitan Museum is supposed to have four oliphants in all, but I have no information on a fourth one.

441.37 Paris, Bibliothèque Nationale, Cabinet des Medailles (formerly in the collection of the Duke of Luynes; originally in the Chartreuse de Portes (Ain)). About 70 cm. long. Mouthpiece end plain; five encircling bands with real and fantastic animals and birds, a rider and a good shepherd. Cahier (1874), 36–41 (with engravings; wrongly identified as the Angers horn); Collaer (1960), 33 (photo); Dufourcq (1946), 42 (photo); Falke (1929–30), 41, and Fig. 6; Harrison (1964), Fig. 36; Swarzenski (1962), 31–40 (photos 35–36); photo Tardy (1966), p. 224.

441.38 Paris, Bibliothèque Nationale, Cabinet des Medailles. No special provision for suspension rings; decorated with a frieze at mouthpiece end. Kühnel (1959), 36.

441.39 Paris, Bibliothèque Nationale, Cabinet des Medailles. About 44 cm. long. Mouthpiece end plain; a frieze of fantastic animals just inside the mouthpiece-end suspension band; the rest of the middle has shallow facets; at bell end, cut off in the middle of a frieze of birds. The Cabinet's catalogue lists Nos. 47–52 as oliphants, but I have information only on the three listed here and 442.19.

441.40 Paris, Louvre (formerly Revoil collection). At mouthpiece and bell ends, procession of animals in circles; in middle, animals in a net of circles. Buhle (1903), 103; Falke (1929–30), 511; Glück (1925), pl. p. 500, bottom; Kühnel (1959), 37, 40, and Fig. 9; Molinier (1896, *Histoire*), 93–94 (with engravings).

441.41 Paris, Louvre (Sauvageot gift, 1856). Short, narrow European copy of the Islamic type. Middle covered with animals in a net of foliage. Falke (1929–30), 517; Glück (1925), pl. p. 500, top; Kühnel (1959), 46.

441.42 Paris, Louvre (earlier in Baron collection). Middle faceted; at bell, a frieze of animals; broken on outside of bell. Kühnel (1959), 36, and Fig. 4; Molinier (1898), 482, and photo p. 483.

441.43 Paris, Musée de Cluny. Length 49 cm., diameter 11 cm. at bell. At mouthpiece and bell, a frieze of animals in circles; in middle, animals in a net of circles; a metal rim at bell; photo Tardy (1966), p. 223.

441.44 Paris, Musée de Cluny, 13065 (originally from Metz; formerly Paris, Spitzer collection; earlier Metz, Colchen collection, until 1867).

Length 64 cm., diameter 12 cm. at bell. Middle decorated with Christ's ascension, evangelists, twelve saints, beasts. Buhle (1903), 103; Cahier (1874), 43–48 (with engravings); Falke (1929–30), 516, and Fig. 8; Kühnel (1959), 49–50, and Fig. 21; Kunz (1916), pl. opp. p. 63, No. III. The Musée de Cluny has six oliphants altogether; those not listed here are evidently post-medieval or African (see Closson (1926), 453).

441.45 Paris, Musée d'Artillerie (in 1903). Buhle (1903), 103.

441.46 Prague, Treasury of St. Vitus' Cathedral (formerly in Karlstein Castle; obtained by Emperor Charles IV in Nonnenwerth Convent, near Rolandseck, Germany). At mouthpiece end, four narrow bands of designs; in middle, four broad bands with quadriga race, hunting scene, mythical beasts, a warrior, etc.; a decorative band at bell end cut off(?). Iron suspension bands and chain. Buchner (1956), Figs. 88–89; Buhle (1903), 103; Dalton (1914), passim; Falke (1929–30), 39–40, and Fig. 1; photo Karstädt (1964), Pl. II.

441.47 Prague, Treasury of St. Vitus' Cathedral (origin same as 441.46). Mouthpiece end plain; a wide band of abstract, interwoven designs around first suspension band; middle plain, unfaceted; a wide band with foliage and grapes inside suspension band; horses and riders at bell. Iron suspension bands and chain. Buchner (1956), Figs. 90–91; Dalton (1914), passim; Falke (1929–30), 41.

441.48 Location unknown (formerly Riga, collection of Baron von der Recke). At ends, frieze of animals in circles; in middle, lengthwise bands with processions of animals. Kühnel (1959), 43–44.

441.49 St. Hubert, Luxemburg Province, Belgium, Abbey Church of St. Hubert. Supposed to have belonged to St. Hubert (fl. early eighth century). Metal fittings. Closson (1926), 455.

441.50 Salisbury (or Winchester Castle?). Mouthpiece end and middle smooth; at bell, a rather narrow frieze with two sphinxes, lion, wild boar, animal with head broken away, griffon. Cahier (1874), 49, and engravings 49 and 50.

441.51 Saragossa, Cathedral of Maria del Pilar. Middle has four crosswise decorated bands, all curiously parallel to the top carrying band; the bell end apparently crudely cut off at the top of the decorative band above the carrying band. Buhle (1903), 104; Falke (1929–30), 44; Goldron (1968), Fig. 21, p. 26, and Fig. 24, p. 27; Swarzenski (1962), 40–42, and Figs. 19–21.

441.52 Stockholm, Nationalmuseum. Animals in a net of circles. Falke (1929–30), 511, and Fig. 1; Kühnel (1959), 37.

441.53 Stralsund, Kulturhistorisches Museum (in 1903). Buhle (1903), 104.

441.54 Toulouse, Musée (in 1839 in the Treasury of St. Sernin's Church). Mouthpiece end plain; in middle, four circumferential bands with a good shepherd and mostly fantastic beasts; at bell, a band of beasts, the half inside the horn's curve cut off down to suspension band. Buhle (1903), 104; Swarzenski (1962), 40, and Figs. 22–24; photo Tardy (1966), p. 221.

441.55 Vienna, collection of Dr. Albert Figdor (in 1930). Fabulous animals in four circumferential bands. Falke (1929–30), 41, and Fig. 7; Swarzenski (1962), 31, 41.

441.56 Vienna, Kunsthistorisches Museum, Ambras Collection, A. 283. Length 48 cm. Broken at one side of mouthpiece; evidently cut off at mouthpiece. Mouthpiece end plain; in middle, animals in a loose net of foliage; at bell end, a procession of animals. Falke (1929–30), 516; Karstädt (1957), photo cols. 745–746; Kühnel (1959), 37, 41; Schlosser (1920), 97, and Pl. 48.

441.57 Vienna, Kunsthistorisches Museum, S. 284 (from Muri Monastery, Switzerland). Length 51.8 cm. Produces the notes g and c' (sharp). Mouthpiece end plain; in middle, 16 lengthwise facets covered with a late, fake inscription; at bell end, a frieze of unicorn, lion, hunter, dog, deer, griffon, basilisks. Closson (1926), 454; Falke (1929–30), 41–42; Geiringer (1943), Pl. IV, No. 2; Gessler (1925), 92, 168–171 (photo 169); Kinsky (1929), p. 43, Fig. 2; Schlosser (1920), 97, and Pl. 48; Schlosser (1922), Pl. 24, No. 78; Swarzenski (1962), 34, and Figs. 12–13.

441.58 York, Chapter House of York Minster. The "horn of Ulph," according to a fairly reliable tradition, the symbol of tenure of lands, and given with them to the Minster by Ulph Thoroldsson before 1042. Length 71 cm., diameter 13 cm. at bell. Mouthpiece end plain; middle faceted; at bell, a procession of animals with foliage: two griffons, a unicorn, an animal combat, a small quadruped. Bridge (1905), 119–121, and pl. opp. p. 119; Gale (1804); Kendrick (1937); Kunz (1916), 45–47; Pegge (1786), passim; Swarzenski (1962), 34, and Figs. 10–11.

441.59 Zürich, Schweizerisches Landesmuseum. Given to the Abbey of St. Gall by St. Norbert, "presumably before his retirement in 1072." Length 56 cm., diameter 11 cm. at bell. In middle, about 15 lengthwise facets; frieze at bell end. Buhle (1903), 104; Falke (1929–30), 42; Gessler (1925), 92–94 (photo 93), 170–171; Kendrick (1937), 281; Swarzenski (1962), 43.

441.60 Scotland, private collection (in 1858). At mouthpiece, a frieze of animals in circles; in middle, lengthwise bands with animals in procession; at bell, a frieze of lion hunters. Falke (1929–30), 511; Kühnel (1959), 44; Waring (1858), Pl. 3.

442. LATER IVORY HORNS
After the eleventh century, the making of ivory horns quickly ceased to be a big industry, but isolated examples, at least, have been turned out

ever since. After the relative homogeneity of the classic oliphants, the later ones have nothing in common, except perhaps the care and artistry that ivory has always demanded of those who work in it.

442.01 Berlin, Staatliche Museen (in 1930 Berlin, Kaiser-Friedrich-Museum). Thirteenth century. South Italian or Sicilian, with suggestions of eleventh-century motifs. At the ends, stylized foliage, animals, human heads; in the middle, about ten lengthwise facets; inside each suspension band a pseudo-Kufic inscription. Falke (1929–30), 44, with Fig. 9; Kendrick (1937), 281; photo Tardy (1966), p. 223.

442.02 Brussels, Musées Royaux d'Art et d'Historie. Thirteenth century, probably Norwegian. Walrus ivory. From mouthpiece end nearly to the middle, about seven lengthwise facets; on bell half, four bands with woven figures, stylized foliage, faces. Bull (1929), II, 125 (photo).

442.03 Brussels, Musée d'Armes et d'Armures de la Porte de Hal, Series 11, No. 1. Thirteenth century. Decorated with foliage and fantastic animals. Closson (1926), 455.

442.04 Clermont-Ferrand (Puy-de-Dôme), Musée Bargouin (supposed to have come from the cathedral of Clermont-Ferrand). Attributed to the eleventh or twelfth century. The very broad mouthpiece end has a metal cap decorated with a lengthwise band on each facet, each with two facing birds or animals. The middle is plain, except for about eight lengthwise facets; there are no suspension bands. At the bell end, a horizontal band with animals and birds. Photo Tardy (1966), p. 224.

442.04A Copenhagen, Carl Claudius Collection, 501 (457). Nearly identical to No. 442.09; perhaps a later copy of it. The six escutcheons are ivory, and blank. Length 50 cm. Two suspension rings attached to the inside curve. Skjerne (1931), 300–301, and photo p. 299.

442.05 Crathes Castle, Kincardineshire, collection of Sir James Home Burnett (in 1905). The Crathes tenure horn. Mounted with gilt silver. A drinking horn(?). Maskell (1905), 243–244; Williamson (1938), 165–166.

442.06 Florence, Museo Nazionale, Carrand Collection, 67. Norwegian, twelfth century. Walrus ivory: 24.5 cm. long. Divided lengthwise into six sections, two of which are plain except for the inscription "MAVRICIVS" on one; the other four have animals mixed with foliage, probably with influence of the Islamic horns. Photo *Enciclopedia Italiana* 11 (1931), 436, bottom, No. 1; Goldschmidt (1914–26), III, No. 140, pp. 38–39, and Pl. XLVIII.

442.07 Florence, Museo Nazionale, Carrand Collection, 39. Norwegian, ca. 1200. Supposedly belonged to Rollo, Duke of Normandy (879–927). Walrus ivory: 52 cm. long; rectangular cross section. At the mouthpiece end a runic inscription "Reinaldr(?) made me," and an animal head, out of which the decoration (on the two broad sides) grows; decoration of fantastic intertwined animals. A signal horn(?). Photo *Enciclopedia Italiana* 11 (1931), 436, top, No. 1; Goldschmidt (1914–26), III, No. 141, p. 39, and Pl. XLVIII.

442.08 Florence, Museo Nazionale. German, fourteenth century. Spiral shape, like a bovine horn. Intricately carved all over with geometric designs. Photo *Enciclopedia Italiana* 11 (1931), 436, top, No. 2.

442.09 Gotha, Schlossmuseum. Made for Christian I of Oldenburg, King of Denmark, Norway and Sweden (1448–81). Extremely intricate carving of hunting on horseback, knights killing a dragon and a giant bird, and jousting; equally intricate gold bands at the ends, middle, and down the inside and outside curves; six small silver escutcheons have the arms of Denmark, Norway, Sweden and others. Koechlin (1924), I, 459, and III, Pl. CCVI, No. 1248a; small photo *Meyers Neues Lexikon* 6 (Leipzig, 1964), 260; Skjerne (1931), 300–301.

442.10 London, Victoria and Albert Museum, 8035–1862. Twelfth century, or later(?). (Engel and Longhurst believed it a classic oliphant.) Length 53 cm., diameter at bell 11.5 cm. Eight facets extend for the whole length of the horn; they are mostly smooth, with no place for suspension bands. Evidently once had a separate (metal?) mouthpiece. Near the mouthpiece end, a rectangle on each facet, each with a man or animal; in the middle of the inside curve, a naked man on horseback blowing a horn; near the bell end, a medallion on each facet, with a cross, animals, and men. Engel (1874), 228; Kendrick (1937), 281; Longhurst (1927–29), I, 51, and Pl. XXVI, middle and bottom; Maskell (1905), 424, and Pl. LI, No. 1; photo Tardy (1966), p. 224.

442.11 London, Victoria and Albert Museum, A 564–1910 (Salting bequest; earlier in Londesborough collection, No. 777 of the 1888 sale catalogue). Beginning of the fourteenth century (or possibly nineteenth century). At the mouthpiece, a female head; in the middle, about twelve lengthwise facets; at the bell, a band with scenes from the life of St. Eustache, riding with horn at mouth, kneeling before deer, leaving his family for exile. With engraved silver suspension bands, joined by lengthwise bands supporting six escutcheons with the arms of Bohemia, Austria, and Bavaria. Koechlin (1924), I, 459–460, II, 436, III, Pl. CCV, No. 1248; Longhurst (1927–29), II, 51–52, with photo Fig. 5.

442.12 London, Victoria and Albert Museum, 7954–1862 (formerly in the Soltikoff collection, No. 377 of the 1861 sale catalogue). German, late fifteenth or sixteenth century. Length 66.5 cm., diameter 13 cm. at the bell. Mouthpiece and bell of metal. Ornately decorated in about nine bands running the whole length, with hunting scenes, St. Christopher, fantastic scenes, much foliage. Two suspension holes on the inside curve, as part of the body itself. Engel (1874), 228, (with engraving); Gay (1877–1928), I, 423 (engraving); Longhurst (1927–29), II, 88, with photo Fig. 6; Maskell (1905), 243, and Pl. LI, No. 2; Molinier (1896, *Histoire*), 197; photo (detail) Tardy (1966), p. 140.

442.13 Lucerne, collection of Ernst and Marthe Kofler-Truniger, S 52. German or Italian, probably thirteenth or fourteenth century. Length 16.7 cm. The preserved portion seems to be the bell end, with a tenon for attachment of a separate bell. Octagonal(?) cross section; decorated with eight circumferential bands: (from the smaller end) rope, eggs, quatrefoils, ovals, quatrefoils, vines, leaves, eggs. The designs are cut shallowly, and the cuts blackened. Schnitzler (1964), 20, and unnumbered plate.

442.14 Maastricht, Treasury of St. Servatius. Fourteenth or fifteenth century. The ivory is decorated only with ten facets running the whole length. Mounted with silver, gilt and enameled, in four circumferential bands, and strips along the inner and outer curves, with a suspension chain attached to the two inner bands; the inner bands have an inscription, the outer ones have hunting scenes. Bock (1872), Fig. 38, p. 303; Koechlin (1924), I, 460, II, 436, III, Pl. CCVI, No. 1249.

442.15–17 Maastricht, Treasury of St. Servatius. Three other oliphants, on which I have no information. Bock (1872), 103, 123; Gessler (1925), 91.

442.18 Munich, Bayerisches Nationalmuseum, A 9396. Central Europe, thirteenth century. In two parts; faceted surface; painted red inside. Ott (1951), 71.

442.19 Paris, Bibliothèque Nationale, Cabinet des Medailles. Fourteenth century(?). Walrus ivory(?). About 40 cm. long, 9 cm. in diameter at the bell. Mouthpiece flared; an extension on the middle of the inside curve has a suspension hole. Nine lengthwise facets, each carved with ropes, foliage, flowers, acorns, monkeys(?), hunters, dogs, and a deer, etc. Engraving Goldron (1968), p. 26, No. 22; photo Tardy (1966), 221.

442.20 Savernake, Marlborough, Wilts, collection of the Marquess of Aylesbury (in 1937 and earlier). The "Bruce horn," said to have been the symbol of the holding of Savernake forest. Length 61 cm., diameter at the bell 14 cm. The ivory itself has no decoration other than sixteen lengthwise facets. It has fine fourteenth-century enameled, silver-gilt fittings: a band around the bell end, two suspension bands, and a mouthpiece. At the bell, on the end: sixteen falcons; around the side: a bishop, king, and hunter (Turpin, Charlemagne, and Roland?), seven dogs, lion, hare, three deer, unicorn. The suspension bands also have figures, or animals and birds. The carrying band, with figured metal mounts, is probably of the same date. Jones (1909), 222; Karstädt (1964), 34, and Pl. V (after Lacroix); Kendrick (1937), 281–282; Lacroix (1874), Fig. 145–146 (after Pegge); Pegge (1786), 24–29, and Pl. VI; Watts (1928), 277.

442.21 Sigmaringen, Hohenzollern collection (in 1876). Thirteenth-fifteenth century(?). Extremely rich carving. Buhle (1903), 104; Koechlin (1924), I, 459.

443. BOVINE HORNS

It is natural to assume that aurochs and other bovine horns were the original musical horns, and continued in use alongside the horns of other materials that imitate their shape. But, although bovine horns fitted for use as drinking horns have been preserved and excavated in very large numbers, there are few medieval bovine horns that were definitely intended to produce sounds.

443.1 Cologne, Treasury of St. Severin. The "Corneliushorn," used as a reliquary, and displayed every Monday at the "Hörnchenmesse." From the illustrations, evidently a steer horn; decorated with metal mounts and jewels. According to Gay, from the fourteenth century. Not a musical horn(?). Gay (1887–1928), I, 428, and II, 169 (engravings); Maskell (1905), 240.

443.2 London, Victoria and Albert Museum (acquired 1938; until 1935 in the possession of the Pusey family). According to tradition, given by Canute (King of England, 1016–35) as a symbol of tenure of the Pusey estate. Length 62 cm. The gilt silver mounting dates from about 1440; it consists of a narrow band at the bell, a band in the middle with the inscription "Kyng Knoude geve wyllyam pewse thys horne to holde by thy lond," and two feet on the middle band. Has a removable plug, for conversion from a drinking to a signal horn. Jones (1909); Kendrick (1937), 279, 282; Pegge (1786), Pl. II and passim; Stone (1961), 104 (with photo).

443.3 Falun, Dala fornsal (now Dalarnas Museum?), 7279. Excavated in 1937 in a peat bog in Sandbäckmyran, Hedemora Parish, Dalarna Province, Sweden. From Viking period (about tenth century). Horn probably from a cross between aurochs and *Bos taurus brachyseros* (a variety of domesticated cattle). Length 22.2 cm., largest diameter 5.7 cm. Has four finger holes on the outside curve, giving the notes e'' flat, e'', f'', g'', a'' (elsewhere d'', d'' sharp, e'', f'', f'' sharp). Oldeberg (1950), 26–27, 45, and Figs. 4–5; Oldeberg (1952), 149–151.

443.4 London, The Wallace Collection, 111. J. 499. Probably German, late fifteenth century. Length 45 cm. Baines: "The Horn of Saint Hubert, given by Louis of Bourbon to Charles the Bold after 1468. Horn, encrusted with gesso painted and gilt, with silver bands decorated with enamel." Baines (1966), 128, and Fig. 692.

444. WOOD HORNS AND MOUTHPIECES

444.1 Excavated in 1920 with the ship at Kvalsund, Nerlandsö, Herøy, Sunmøre, Norway. About A.D. 600. A conical wood pipe, about 72 cm. long; the diameter at the small end is 4 cm., and thus it is very possible that the object is for shouting, rather than playing. Oldeberg (1950), 58; Oldeberg (1952), 151; Shetelig (1929), 30 ff., and Figs. 18–19, p. 56.

444.2 Bygdøy, Oslo, Vikingskipshuset. Object No. 152 from the Oseberg ship of ca. A.D. 850. A generally cylindrical tube of beechwood or yew, 107 cm. long. The outer cross section is elliptical, about 3–4 cm. across; the inner is squarish, about 2 x 2 cm. The tube is made of two split halves, hollowed out; five shallow bands are cut into the outside, which probably held the bindings that held the two halves together. A rim cut into the small end suggests a mouthpiece. Brøgger (1917–28), II, 270–271, with Fig. 165, English p. 356; Sevåg (1966), cols. 9–10, with two photos.

444.3   Birmingham, Weoley Castle Museum. A wood mouthpiece of a trumpet, horn or bagpipe, excavated at Weoley Castle, and dating from about 1260. Burchard (1965).

444.4   A wood horn or trumpet mouthpiece, excavated at Wolin, Poland. Kamiński (1968), 19 (with drawings), dates it in the mid-ninth century; p. 39, dates it ninth to thirteenth century.

445. CERAMIC HORNS

To judge from the number of specimens found, in Germany, at least, pottery horns may have been the commonest type for everyday signaling purposes in the Middle Ages.

445.1   Terra-cotta horn found at Quivillon (Seine-Maritime). Fourteenth century. Length 15 cm. Behind the mouthpiece, a 270-degree curve in the tube, so that the bell is at a 90-degree angle to the mouthpiece end. *Larousse* (1957), I, 229 (photo).

445.2   Fragments of one or more horns, excavated in 1849 in the ruins of Tannenberg Castle, near Darmstadt. The castle was built about 1200, and destroyed in 1399. Brick-red pottery: length about 42.2 cm., width at bell about 11.6 cm. Curved in the shape of a bovine horn; nine lengthwise facets; flared bell. Hefner (1850), 88, and Pl. VI, K (a reconstruction based on the fragments of 445.2 and 3).

445.3   Fragments of one or more horns, excavated in Daxberg Castle (evidently the same as the Tagisberg, excavated in 1848), near Darmstadt. Hefner (1850), 88.

445.4+   Langerwehe, near Düren (Nordrhein-Westfalen), Töpferei-Museum (for one example, see Fig. 28). The museum has several horns, made by Langerwehe potters in the late Middle Ages (and probably somewhat later), and fragments continue to be dug up in the vicinity. They were called *Aach-, Pilger-, Heiligtums-* and *Wetterhörner,* the first three names referring to an association with pilgrimages to Aachen (Virdung illustrates an *Acher horn* with its carrying strap in *Musica getutscht* (1511), fol. D3 verso). These horns are in the usual horn shape, from 25 to 50 cm. long. The mouthpiece, and sometimes the bell, is flared; there are from two to four loops for suspension, sometimes with pottery rings in them. Decoration consists of lengthwise facets shaved off the sides of the horn before firing (very possibly in imitation of the typical oliphant facets, or even specifically copying those of the Aachen oliphant), and green or yellow glaze at the bell end. Schwarz (1935).

446. GLASS HORNS

It is possible that all of these objects are drinking glasses in the shape of signal horns, in other words, closed at the mouthpiece end to hold beverages.

446.1   Found at Stangeland, Haaland District, Stavanger County, Norway. From the late Iron Age(?). Fragments of a glass drinking horn (closed at the mouthpiece end) in the shape of a signal horn, with flared mouthpiece and bell. Decorated with threads; a suspension loop on the inside curve. The middle portion is missing. Gustafson (1906), 81, and Fig. 380; Rygh (1885), 17, Fig. 339; Skjerne (1931–39), 306.

446.2   Copenhagen, Nationalmuseet, C 19668. Found at Lærkenfelt Mark, Hansted Parish, Vor District, Aarhus County, Denmark. Rhenish fabrication, from the Migration period. Closed at the small end, in the shape of a mouthpiece. Skjerne (1931–39), 305–306.

446.3   London, British Museum. From a Frankish grave of the fifth or sixth century at Bingerbrück, Rhineland. In the shape of a horn, with flared mouthpiece. Decorated with glass threads on the surface. Two heavier loops on the inside curve, for suspension. Reportedly a drinking glass in the form of a signal horn. Photo *Encyclopædia Britannica*, 11th ed. (1910–11), vol. 8, pl. opp. p. 582, Fig. 4; photo Rice (1965, *Dark Ages*), 200.

446.4   Collection of Victor Gay (in 1887). Identified as fourteenth-century glassware from the Meuse. Flared mouthpiece; decorated with encircling threads and ruffles. Gay (1887–1928), I, 422 (engraving).

447. COPPER, BRONZE, BRASS HORNS

The common medieval copper-alloy horns represent a rather distinct type. Like almost every one of the instruments of types 441–448, they curve gently from mouthpiece to bell, the usual curve being 45–60 degrees, although some are a little over 90 degrees. The bore is strictly conical, except for an occasional cylindrical mouthpiece end, and a more rapidly widening bore near the bell, sometimes even a pronounced flaring. There are usually suspension loops, commonly two on the inside curve.

Numbers 02–11 of the present list are the so-called "burgmote" horns, used to call meetings of the British corporation councils, and still mostly in possession of the corporations. I do not know of reliable dates for them, although they seem to conform to the late medieval type. There may be others in addition to those listed here. A careful examination of these instruments and the records of their use would be very desirable.

447.01   Dover, Dover Castle Keep. Saxon or Norman(?). About 51 cm. long. Bridge (1905), 139.

447.02   Dover, Corporation of Dover (Fig. 29). Thirteenth-century(?). Bronze or brass: 81 cm. long, 13 cm. diameter at bell. Jewitt: "deeply chased with a kind of spiral scroll-work of foliage, and other ornaments on a hatched ground. On an encircling band, four inches from the mouth, and a spiral continuation starting from it," the inscription ".A.G.L.A.Johannes de.Allemaine.me.fecit." (AGLA stands for the Hebrew formula "Thou art mighty for ever, O Lord!") Hipkins (1888), xiii, 1–2, and Pl. I (shorter horn); Jewitt (1880), 255; Skjerne (1931–39), 339 (illustration after Hipkins).

447.03   Faversham, Corporation of Faversham(?). Bridge (1905), 138–139.

447.04   Folkestone, Kent, Corporation of Folkestone(?). Brass: 91 cm. long. Engraved at bell: "FOVLSTAN." Galpin (1911, 4th ed.), 139; Jewitt (1880) (mention).

447.05   Hythe, Kent, Corporation of Hythe(?). Galpin (1911, 4th ed.), 139 (mention).

447.06   Ipswich, East Suffolk, Corporation of Ipswich. Supposed to be from the reign of King John (1199–1216). Length 83 cm. Galpin (1911, 4th ed.), 139; Jewitt (1880), 255.

447.07   London, Guildhall. The Canterbury burgmote horn. Brass: 93 cm. long, 14 cm. in diameter at bell, 2 cm. in diameter at mouthpiece end. Two suspension loops on inside curve; no inscription or ornament. Records report use of this or a similar horn for calling meetings of the Corporation since 1376. Bridge (1905), 139; Galpin (1911, 4th ed.), 139; Hipkins (1888), xiii, 1–2, and Pl. I (longer horn); Jewitt (1880), 253.

447.08   New Romney, Kent, Corporation of New Romney(?). Bridge (1905), 139; Jewitt (1880) (mention).

447.09   Ripon, Yorkshire, "Mayor's horn." Galpin (1911), 188; Jewitt (1880), 255–256.

447.10   Sandwich, Kent, Corporation of Sandwich. Lost(?). Bridge (1905), 140.

447.11   Winchester, Hants, Museum over the Westgate (in 1905). Thirteenth or fourteenth century(?). Only decoration: at the bell end, a relief of four rampant lions, alternating with bishops. Two square loops for suspension. Bridge (1905), 140; Cahier (1874), 41–43, with engraving.

447.12   Berlin, Zeughaus (acquired 1930 or 1931). Fifteenth century. Gilt copper, with ornamented silver bands. The mouthpiece proceeds from an animal's mouth. Suspension rings protrude on the inside curve from two silver bands. Inscribed "Saint Georges Au Bō Duc," presumably indicating a gift of the noble society of St. George of Burgundy to Philip the Good (Duke 1419–62). Closs (1931), with photo, and drawing of inscription.

447.13–14   Lucerne, Historisches Museum. Two "Harschhörner," dated 1495, Lucerne. Gessler (1925), 28–29, with photo of one.

447.15   New Haven, Conn., Yale University Collection of Musical Instruments (on loan from the Belle Skinner Collection, Holyoke, Mass.). Probably southern France, fifteenth century. Gilt copper with a silver rim and silver mouthpiece. Two suspension rings on the inside curve, two on the outside. Length 31.4 cm., diameter at bell 8.8 cm. Embossed with foliage and the repeated letters "ea" on a background of crosshatching. Marcuse (1960), Pl. 25, and unnumbered page.

447.16   Paris, Musée du Conservatoire. Small horn with decoration in relief on the bell; has the name "Andrea," and the date "1420." Chouquet (1884), 142.

447.17   Riga, Cathedral Museum. Fragment of a bronze horn of the Migration Period or early Middle Ages, from the Baltic region. Suspension rings. Behn (1954), 167.

448. OTHER METAL HORNS

448.1   Gold horn found in 1639 at Gallehus, near Møgeltønder and Tondern, Sønderjylland, Slesvig, Denmark. Stolen and melted down in 1802. Variously dated, but the most authoritative datings are between extremes of ca. A.D. 400 and 450. Hartner (1969) argues that this and No. 448.2 were made as charms against the effects of the total eclipse of the sun of 16 April A.D. 413. In the standard curved shape, with gentle taper. The length is divided by removable rings into fourteen sections, seven of which are covered with figures of men and animals in relief. Hartner makes the convincing claim that the figures on the second band from the wide end are really runes; his reading of them as "lupa horns ens helpa hjoho," "May the magic potion of this horn help the clan," is less convincing. A screw-on plug was made in the seventeenth century to convert it to a drinking horn. The Nationalmuseet, Copenhagen, has a fine reconstruction, made in 1860 of gilt silver after drawings and measurements of the original. The Hermitage(?), Leningrad, has an old ivory copy, made from the original. Another reconstruction is in the Musée des Antiquités Nationales, St.-Germain-en-Laye (Yvelines). Andersen (1945); Bibby (1956), 329–338; *Bibliotheca Danica* II (Copenhagen, 1962), cols. 583–585 (bibliography of 23 seventeenth- to early nineteenth-century publications on this and No. 448.2); Bridge (1905), 143, and pl. opp. p. 143; Brix (1949); Brøndsted (1954); Brøndsted (1960), 321–326; Niemeyer (1955, "Germanische Musik"), cols. 1815–1816, and Fig. 2; Oxenstierna (1953); Oxenstierna (1956); Ringbom (1949); Schiørring (1952), col. 1841, and Pl. 62 (the Copenhagen reconstruction); Skjerne (1931–39).

448.2   Gold horn found in 1734 ten paces from No. 448.1. Stolen and melted down in 1802. Danish, of the same date as No. 448.1. In the standard curved shape. At least a third of the horn's length, at the mouthpiece end, was missing when the horn was found. Divided into sections by raised bands. Decoration of men and animals in relief. At the bell, a runic inscription "ek hlewagastir holtijar horna tawido," "I, Lægæst, Holte's son [or: from Holt], made the horn." (The instrument is thus the only medieval one that gives exact evidence as to what name its maker called it.) The Nationalmuseet, Copenhagen, has a silver-gilt reconstruction, lovingly made in 1860 after the drawings and measurements of the original. Another reconstruction is in the Musée des Antiquités Nationales, St.-Germain-en-Laye. Anderson (1938); Baeksted (1947); Bridge (1905), 143, and pl. opp. p. 143; Huyge (1963), Fig. 207 (the Copenhagen reconstruction); Niemeyer (1955, "Germanische Musik"), cols. 1815–1816; Schiørring (1952), col. 1841, and Pl. 62 (the Copenhagen reconstruction); also the other literature under No. 448.1.

448.3   Vienna, Kunsthistorisches Museum. Ninth century. From a large gold treasure found in 1799 in Nagyszentmiklós, Hungary (now Romania; probably by coincidence, Bartók's birthplace). Small, about 20 cm. long; made of two straight parts joined at an angle, with mouthpiece and bell attached. Runic(?) inscription on the bell. The hole at the mouthpiece is only about 3 mm. in diameter; it is questionable whether it was intended as a musical instrument, although it seems to be intentionally in the shape of one. Fleischer (1900), 568; Oxenstierna (1953); Ringbom (1949); Skjerne (1931–39), 298–299.

448.4   Paris, Musée du Conservatoire (from the Clapisson collection). Fifteenth century(?). An iron horn. Chouquet (1884), 142.

449. BUISINES

Only a small number of medieval trumpets are known, all of them of the straight, cylindrical-bore type called buisines or clairons.

449.1   Ann Arbor, Michigan, Stearns Collection, 804 (donated by Francis W. Kelsey). Italian, fifteenth or sixteenth century. Bronze: 131 cm. long, 8.4 cm. in diameter at the bell. "Decorated with engraved bands and bars near the bell." Stanley (1918), 117.

449.2   Boston, Museum of Fine Arts (Fig. 30). By Sebastian Hainlein. The date is given as 1460, but the two Sebastian Hainleins listed by Langwill (1960), 47, as instrument makers in Nürnberg are much later, the first having died in 1631, and the second one living from 1594–1655; Langwill suggests that the date should be MDCLX, not MCDLX. According to Bate (1966), Pl. 10B, "Recent re-examination by an expert Medievalist suggests that the bell section is in fact of 19th-century workmanship, though the rest of the instrument is probably very ancient." Brass: 106.5 cm. long (101.7 cm. without the mouthpiece). Decorated with engraved brass bands; at the bell rim: "MACHT SEBASTIAN HAIN-

LEIN.M.CDLX." One ring for attachment of a banner. Fundamental tone *d*. The mouthpiece is not original. Bessaraboff (1941), 188, and Pl. VII, No. 198; Galpin (1911), 201, and Pl. 41, No. 1.

449.3 Brussels, Musée d'Armes et d'Armures de la Porte de Hal. Fifteenth-seventeenth century(?). About 150 cm. long. A bulb about 30 cm. from the bell; two small rings for a banner.

449.4 Washington, Smithsonian Institution, 95294. Dated 1411. Length 134 cm. Densmore (1927), 46, and Pl. 20a.

449.5 Williamstown, Mass.(?), collection of Mrs. Murray D. Smith. Marked Siena, 1406. Used in the New York Pro Musica recording of *The Play of Daniel* (Decca DL 9402).

449.6 Paris, Musée du Conservatoire. Trumpet (or horn?) mouthpiece, fourteenth century(?). Chouquet (1884), 152.

451. ORGANS

To say that a medieval organ is extant does not mean what it does to say that, for example, a medieval oliphant is extant. Usually, it means "an organ exists, parts of which are from the Middle Ages," or "some parts of a medieval organ exist." For a church organ to be preserved, it must continue to function in a way acceptable to the people using it. The result is a little reconstruction, some conservation, much total destruction and a great deal of authorized vandalism. With all this, a surprising number of organs from before 1500 exist, but hardly any are substantially in their original states.

The present list is surely not complete, and details are sparse, as I have seen good accounts of only a few of the organs. The list includes all the organs I have been able to find reported as existing as recently as the late nineteenth century. Some have been destroyed since they were described; on some others I have no recent information.

451.01 Anga, Gotland, Sweden, Anga Church. Ca. 1400. Klotz (1962); Quoika (1966), 16–17. For more extensive accounts of the Gotland organs, see Erici (1965), and Wester (1936).

451.02 Etelhem, Gotland, Etelhem Church. A fragment of an organ, ca. 1430. Klotz (1962); Quoika (1966), 16.

451.03 Hejnum, Gotland, Hejnum Church. Ca. 1400–30. Klotz (1962); Quoika (1966), 17.

451.04 Stockholm, Statens Historiska Museum (originally in Norrlanda, Gotland, Norrlanda Church). Variously dated from ca. 1370 to the earlier fifteenth century. Only the console is preserved. Hennerberg (1909, 1934); Klotz (1962); Quoika (1966), 16–17; Rautioaho (1967), cols. 694–695, with photo; Riedel (1958), col. 1094.

451.05 Stockholm, Statens Historiska Museum (originally in Sundre, Gotland, Sundre Church). Built by Werner of Brandenburg, ca. 1370.

Only the quasi-cubical case is preserved. Photo Haacke (1965), 5; Hennerberg (1909, 1934); Klotz (1962); Quoika (1966), 16–17; Riedel (1958), cols. 1093–1094.

451.06 Stockholm, Statens Historiska Museum (originally in Knutby, Uppland, Knutby Church). "Chest dated in the later part of the 1400s." Rautioaho (1967), col. 695.

451.07 Bützow (near Rostock), Stadtkirche. Case of ca. 1490 in the west gallery, a new organ in the case in 1618; additions to instrument and case in 1879. Hill (1966), 51–52, 193, and pl. p. 192.

451.08 Dortmund, Marienkirche (destroyed in World War II). Hill: case of ca. 1480, the instrument chiefly recent; Marigold: sixteenth century. Hill (1966), 70, and pl. p. 71; Marigold (1962–63), 81.

451.09 Kiedrich (Rheingau), Church of St. Valentin. The organ has been repaired, altered and rebuilt many times, and contains some elements from every century since the fourteenth (some pipes are dated 1313, and the case may be of the same date, basically). Bösken (1969), 69, 77–78, 81–82, and Pl. 1 and 11; Hill (1966), 52; Marigold (1962–63), 80, 81; Smets (1945, *Kiedrich*); Still (1950–51).

451.10 Lübeck, Marienkirche (destroyed in 1942). Hauptwerk by Johannes Stephani, 1475–77, with positive of 1557–58, in the "Totentanz" Chapel. Hill (1888), with drawing Pl. XVI; Hill (1966), 199, and pl. p. 198; Karstädt (1960), col. 1266, and photo col. 1271; Smets (1945, *Lübeck*), 7–8; Stahl (1932).

451.11 Lübeck, Jakobikirche. Small organ in the south aisle. Hauptwerk from the fifteenth century (Haacke: ca. 1480); Rückpositiv added in 1636–37 by Friedrich Stellwagen of Lübeck; Brustwerk of the seventeenth century; restored and some stops added by Kemper of Lübeck in the twentieth century. Haacke (1965), 17 (photo); Shewring (1959–60), 114–115; Smets (1945, *Lübeck*), 10–11, and photo opp. p. 12.

451.12 Nördlingen, Bavaria, Church of St. Georg. Built in 1466 by Stephan Kaschendorff of Breslau, and reportedly still well preserved. A pedal was added by Kaschendorff in 1486. Konrad Paumann spent several weeks in Nördlingen testing the organ in 1466. Hill (1966), 69–70, and pl. p. 68; Krautwurst (1961); Krautwurst (1964).

451.13 Wissel (near Kleve). Organ case of ca. 1490 and a modern twin, both with new works, played from a console placed between them. Hill (1966), 185, and pl. p. 184.

451.14 Wormbach, Landkreis Meschede, Westphalia, Catholic Parish Church. The organ, built probably shortly after 1700, incorporates old pipes, at least some of which date from the end of the fourteenth century. Later additions and restorations. Reuter (1965), 76–77, and photos Figs. 1 and 96.

451.15 Ossiach (Carinthia), former Benedictine monastery church.

Built about 1450 or somewhat later; rebuilt ca. 1700; much of the original preserved. Owart (1963); Quoika (1966), 25–26.

451.16 Seckau, Obersteiermark, Stiftskirche. Built by Michael Rosenauer during the priorate of Johann Diernberger (1480–1510), or by Hans Pruner in 1500. Modernized in 1715, and removed at the end of the nineteenth century. Since 1905, the prospect has been in the Johanneum, Graz. Eberstaller (1955), 13, 102, 218; Hill (1966), 191, and pl. p. 190.

451.17 Sion, Valais (in German, Sitten, Wallis), Switzerland, Church of Nôtre-Dame de Valère. The original construction is variously dated from ca. 1370 to ca. 1400. The painted shutters reportedly are dated 1437. In 1718 Matthias Carlen of Reckingen added a pedal with its pipes, and other stops. Restored in 1954 by Th. Kuhn of Männedorf. Three of the present eight stops are original. Recordings: Columbia ML 6255 (MS 6855), *E. Power Biggs Plays the Historic Organs of Europe/Switzerland* (with color photo, notes and specifications); Telefunken SAWT 9498B, *Die alte Orgel: Historic Organs of Switzerland.* Haacke (1965), 14 (photo); Hill (1966), 57–59, with pl. p. 58; Klotz (1962), col. 272, and Fig. 32; Münger (1955); Williams (1966), 59, and Pl. 16.

451.18 Groningen, Martinikerk (also called Maartenskerk, Groote Kerk). Built in 1479–82 by Rudolf Agricola. Many later alterations and additions; rebuilt by Arp Schnitger in 1692; little of the original case or works is left. Bouman (1941); Bouman (1949), 35, 36, 48, 62, 119; Kruijs (1885), 15; Vente (1958), 133, 145, 173, 189–190; Williams (1966), 39, 40, 290, 305; Witte (1874–81), 94.

451.19 Middleburg, Koorkerk (originally in Utrecht, Nicolaïkerk; from 1875 (1886?) to 1956 in the Rijksmuseum, Amsterdam). Built in 1477–81 by Peter Gerritsz of Utrecht. Later work in 1547, 1574, 1580 (rugwerk), 1601, 1733. In the nineteenth century all was discarded but the case, front pipes, the Blockwerk chest and some ranks of its pipes, which were installed in the Rijksmuseum. In 1956 it was installed in the Koorkerk, and restored to its original form. Bouman (1949), 18, 19, 30, 35, 37–38, fig. p. 29, and Fig. 1; Klotz (1962), col. 272; *Die Musik in Geschichte und Gegenwart* 13 (1966), cols. 1190–1191, and bibliography col. 1193; Quoika (1966), 33, 38; Riemsdijk (1887); Vente (1958), 13–16, 19, 63, 64, 128, 193, 201, 207, and Figs. 2–7; Williams (1966), 29–30.

451.20 Amiens, Cathedral. Organ over the west entrance to the nave, in its original form completed in 1429. Of the original organ, the base and the case up to the height of the wind chest are preserved. Dufourcq (1969), passim, and Figs. 1, 10, 126; bibliography Fallou (1929), 19; Gastoué (1921), 45–46, 75, and Pl. VI; Hill (1966), 63–64, and pl. p. 62; Servières (1916–17), 466–468, with photo.

451.21 Carcassonne. Servières: some pieces of fifteenth-century woodwork are fitted into a case of the seventeenth and eighteenth centuries.

Dufourcq (1969), 36, 108, and Pl. CVIII; Servières (1916–17), 469–470.

451.22   Chartres, Cathedral. Much of the case of the organ built by Gombert Rogerie ca. 1475 is included in the present state of the organ, and the gallery is largely original. Dufourcq (1969), passim, and Fig. 51; bibliography Fallou (1929), 28–29; Hill (1966), 97–99, with pl. p. 98; Quoika (1966), 48.

451.23   Embrun (Hautes-Alpes), Cathedral. The base of the organ, around and above the console, is from ca. 1480; Dufourcq: only the supporting structure of the gallery is original. Cellier (1964); Dufourcq (1969), passim, with drawing p. 18, and Figs. 2–7; bibliography Fallou (1929), 33; Hill (1966), 193, and pl. p. 192; Servières (1916–17), 468–469.

451.24   Reims, Cathedral. An organ of 1468 was rebuilt in 1487 by Oudin Hestre of Cambrai, after a 1481 fire. After many alterations and rebuildings, part of the 1487 organ remains (the gallery with its balustrade, and some panels of the case). Dufourcq (1969), passim, and Figs. 11, 13, 14, 148; bibliography Fallou (1929), 59; Servières (1916–17), 468, and pl. after p. 468; Wörsching (1946).

451.25   Sacy (Marne), Church of Saint-Rémy (originally in St.-Pierre-le-Vieil, Reims). The gallery and some panels of the case are extant, of the original Gothic organ. Dufourcq (1969), 22, 26, and Fig. 16.

451.26   Solliès-Ville (Var), church. Prospect of a small organ, 2.6 m. high, 2.5 m. wide, inscribed "1499 ista organa fecit frater Antonius Hillani Ordinis Sancti Augustini." All the rest of the organ was removed in the nineteenth century. The woodwork features two sunbursts with faces, the symbol of Solliès. Dufourcq (1969), 20, 26, and Fig. 8; Gensoles (1844–45); Servières (1916–17), 472–473, and photo p. 471; Viollet (1874), 253, 254.

451.27   Strasbourg, Cathedral. The present case was built in 1497 around the organ built in 1489 by Friedrich Krebs (Krebser) of Ansbach, and redecorated in the eighteenth century. Some of the base and the accompanying mechanical sculptures are from the first half of the fourteenth century. The case houses a Roethinger organ of 1935, which replaced one of Andreas Silbermann of 1716. Dufourcq (1969), passim, and Figs. 15, 182, 268, 269; bibliography Fallou (1929), 68; Gass (1935); Gastoué (1921), 46–47; Hill (1966), 75–77, 195, and pl. pp. 74 and 194; Die Musik in Geschichte und Gegenwart 3 (1954), Pl. 38, No. 2; Raugel (1948); Wörsching (1947).

451.28   Vence (Alpes-Maritimes), Cathedral. Hill (1966), 48: "Gothic case of the fifteenth century, now, we believe, disused." Dufourcq (1969), 141, mentions only an eighteenth-century organ.

451.29   Villefranche-de-Rouergue (Aveyron). Organ of 1432, remade in 1508, 1628 and later; still some original elements. Servières (1916–17), 470.

451.30   Bologna, Church of San Petronio. The instrument was built by Lorenzo di Giacomo da Prato in 1470–74, and the case completed in 1483. The organ was repaired in 1513, 1563, 1577, and 1842, and moved to another location in the church in 1659. The case was sheathed in a new one in Baroque style in 1686 (1674?). The organ was restored in 1954 by Tamburini of Crema. Stops have been added at various times, but the original ones are essentially intact. Burns (1960–61); photo Haacke (1965), 15; Hill (1966), 187–189, and pl. p. 186; Klotz (1962), col. 272; Lunelli (1956), 3–11; *Die Musik in Geschichte und Gegenwart 2* (1952), Pl. 5, No. 1; Williams (1966), 205–207, 213, and Pl. 77.

451.31   Cencenighe (Agordino), church. Built between 1478 and 1487 for the Church of San Pietro, Trent. Restored in 1614 by Giovanni Berthe. Sold to Cencenighe in 1852. Demolished in 1953–54 (fragments remained in 1967). Lunelli (1967), 160–162.

451.32   Lucca, Cathedral of San Martino, organ "in cornu Epistolae." Built by Domenico di Lorenzo in 1480–81; additions in 1792. In 1962 the excellently preserved works were removed, and a new organ built, using the old case, and the front pipes as show pipes only. The works are stored in Lucca. Mischiati (1969), 40–43, and pl. opp. p. 48.

451.33   Palma, Majorca, Cathedral. A large organ of ca. 1420 in one of the northern chapels. Adcock (1953–55), 162–163; Hill (1966), 185, and pl. p. 184.

451.34   Alcalá de Henares, Cathedral (destroyed in the Spanish Civil War). Organ of ca. 1450, its case still intact in 1883. Adcock (1953–55), 163; Hill (1966), 67, and pl. p. 66; Vente (1954–58), 156.

451.35   Catalayud (near Saragossa), Church of San Andrés. Organ of ca. 1420. Hill (1912–13), 487.

451.36   Catalayud, Church of Santa María. Organ of ca. 1420. Hill (1912–13), 487.

451.37   Daroca, Church of the Santos Corporales. Organ of ca. 1420 in a gallery at the east end of the church. Hill (1912–13), 487, 488.

451.38   Salamanca, Catedral Vieja (now a museum). An organ in its old gallery in the chapel of San Bartolomé, attached to the cathedral, dated ca. 1380 by Hill, in the second half of the fifteenth century by Vente. The 235 pipes were removed near the end of the nineteenth century. Adcock (1953–55), 162; photo Haacke (1965), 13; Hill (1966), 179, and pl. p. 178; Vente (1954–58), 164.

451.39   Saragossa, Cathedral La Seo. Built in an arch on the south side of the choir, with two faces. Hill: 1413; Vente: 1443. The pipes are mostly of the eighteenth and nineteenth centuries. Adcock (1953–55), 161–162;

Hill (1966), 55, 181, and pl. p. 180; Vente (1954–58), 210, and pl. opp. p. 164; Williams (1966), 235, and Pl. 87.

451.40   Saragossa, Church of San Pablo. Organ of ca. 1420, much altered internally, but still with some fifteenth-century pipes (Hill). Side turrets added in the nineteenth century. Adcock (1953–55), 162; Hill (1966), 183, and pl. p. 182; Vente (1954–58), 210.

451.41   Brussels, Musée Instrumental(?) (in 1884 in the collection of Count Giovanni Correr, Venice). Remains of a small organ by Lorenzo Gusnaschi of Pavia, dated 1494. Boalch (1956), 39.

ILLUSTRATIONS

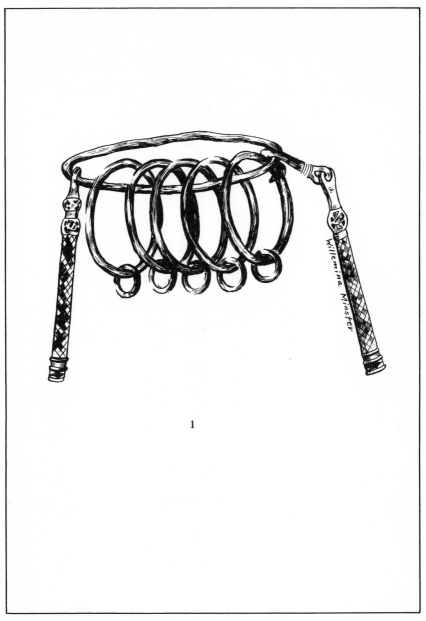

Figure 1. *Type 112.* Rangle from the Oseberg ship burial, ca. A.D. 850.

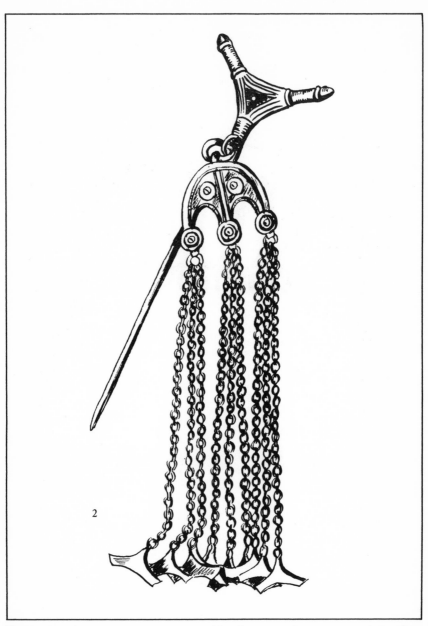

Figure 2. *Type 113*. Bronze pin with silver-coated pendant and dangling bronze jingles. Pin 22.5 cm. long. Ninth century. From Laiviai, Salantai district, Lithuania. Vilnius, Istorijos-etnografijos Muziejus.

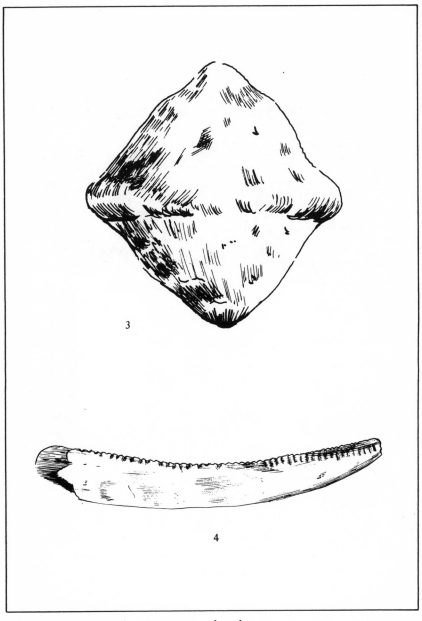

3

4

Figure 3.   *No. 114.15.*   Ceramic vessel rattle.
Figure 4.   *No. 115.2.*   Bone scraper.

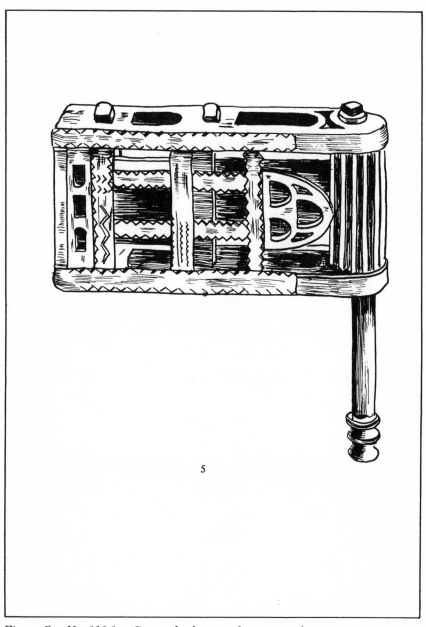

5

Figure 5. *No. 116.1.* Cog rattle, fourteenth to sixteenth century.

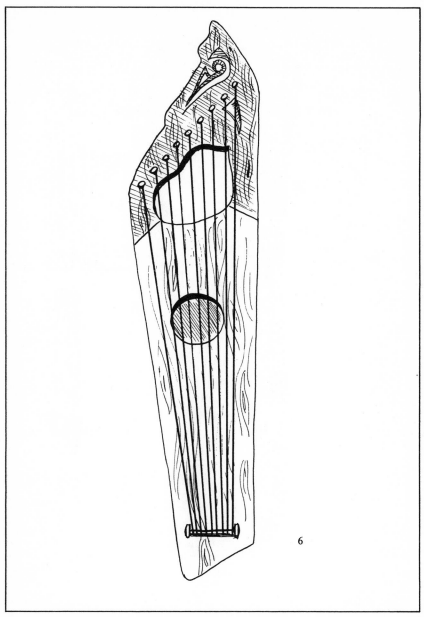

Figure 6.   *No. 312.3.*   Gusli of the thirteenth century from Novgorod, reconstructed.

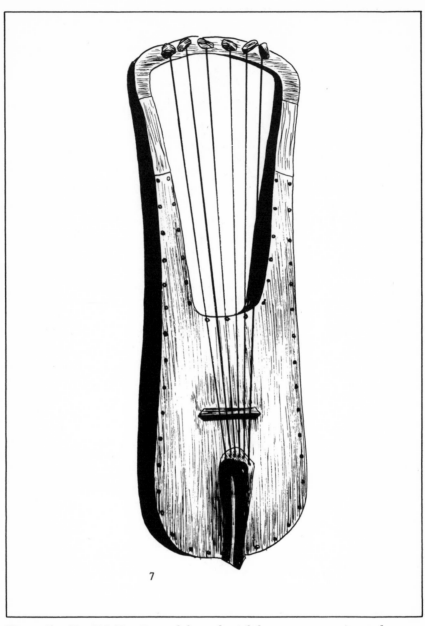

7

Figure 7.   *No. 313.03.*   Lyre of the early eighth century, reconstructed.

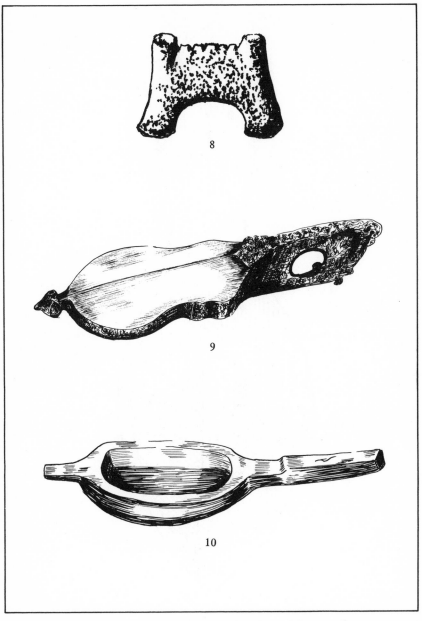

Figure 8.   *No. 313.12.*   Amber lyre bridge of the eighth or ninth century.
Figure 9.   *No. 322.1.*   Gittern, ca. 1300-30.
Figure 10.   *No. 323.1.*   Lute, ca. A.D. 1000.

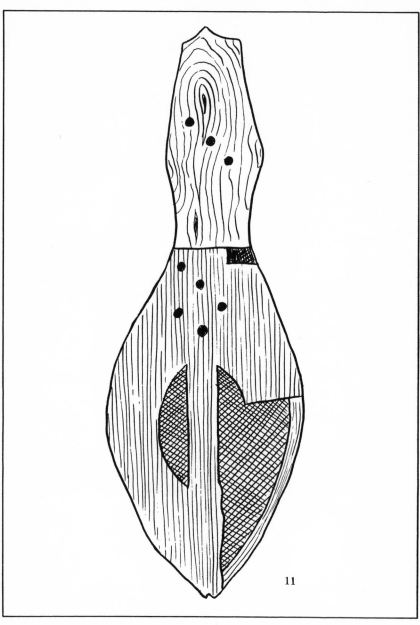

11

Figure 11.   *No. 331.3.*   Fiddle of the fourteenth century from Novgorod.

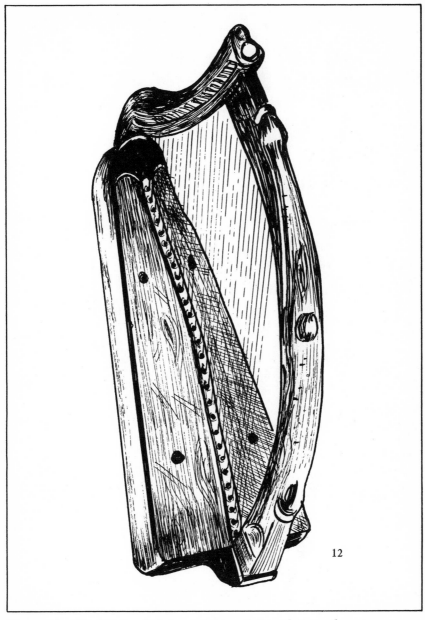

12

Figure 12.   *No. 341.1.*   Irish harp, fourteenth to mid-sixteenth century.

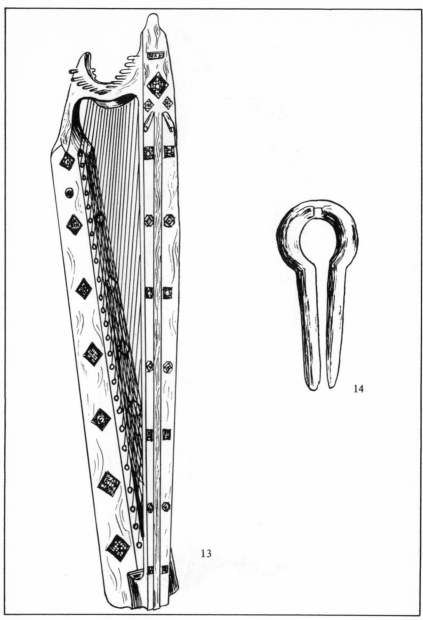

Figure 13. *No. 342.1.* Gothic harp, Tirol, fourteenth or fifteenth century.
Figure 14. *No. 411.03.* Jew's harp, Anglo-Saxon, sixth century (?).

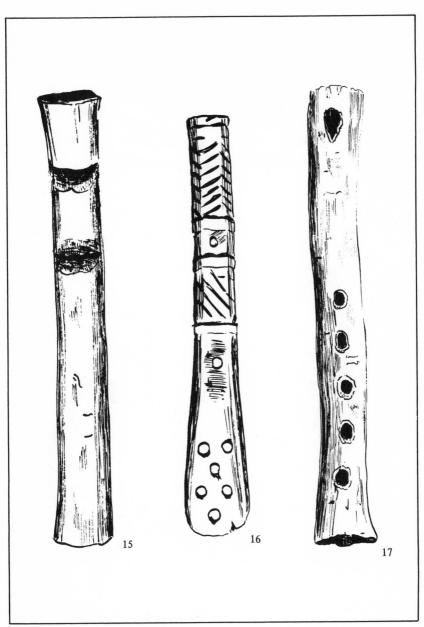

Figure 15. *No. 4211.02.* Bone whistle.
Figure 16. *No. 4212.04.* Bone whistle, first "Frisian" type.
Figure 17. *No. 4213.026.* Bone flute.

83

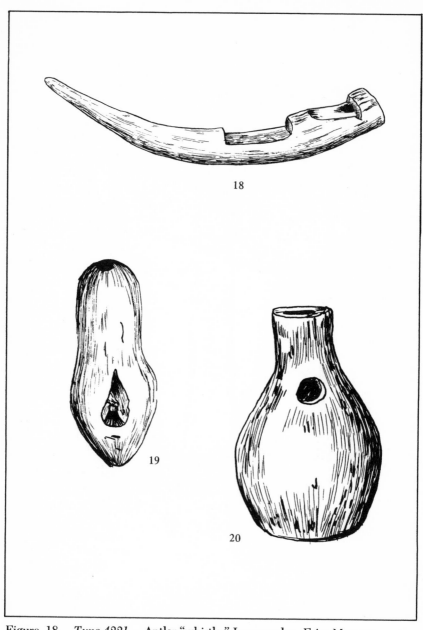

Figure 18. *Type 4221.* Antler "whistle," Leeuwarden, Fries Museum.

Figure 19. *No. 4241.2.* Ceramic whistle.

Figure 20. *No. 4242.1.* Ceramic globular flute, thirteenth or fourteenth century.

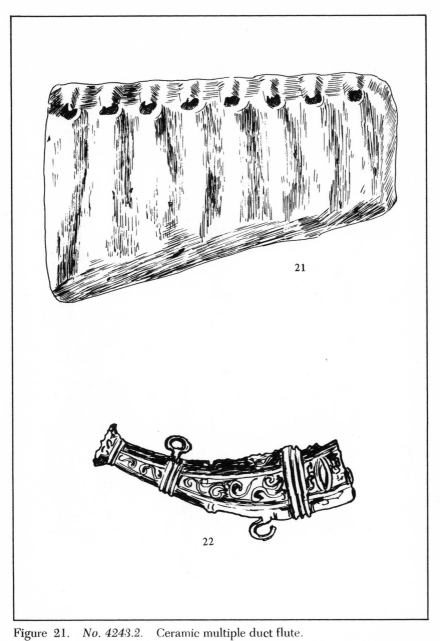

Figure 21.   *No. 4243.2.*   Ceramic multiple duct flute.
Figure 22.   *No. 4251.05.*   Metal whistle, fourteenth or fifteenth century.

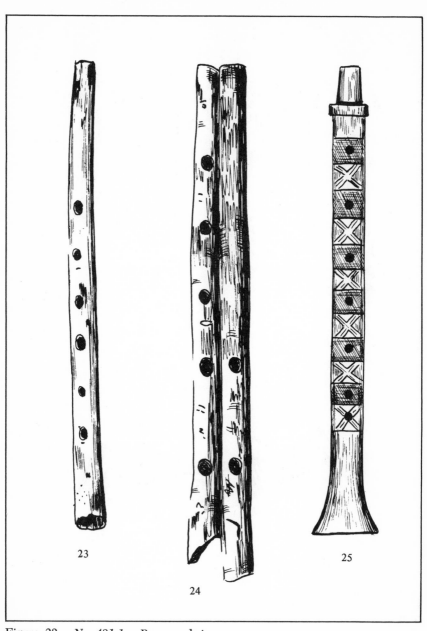

23

24

25

Figure 23. *No. 431.1.* Bone reed pipe.

Figure 24. *No. 432.1.* Bone double reed pipe, seventh to mid-eighth century.

Figure 25. *No. 433.1.* Wood shawm, mid-eighth to eleventh century, reconstructed.

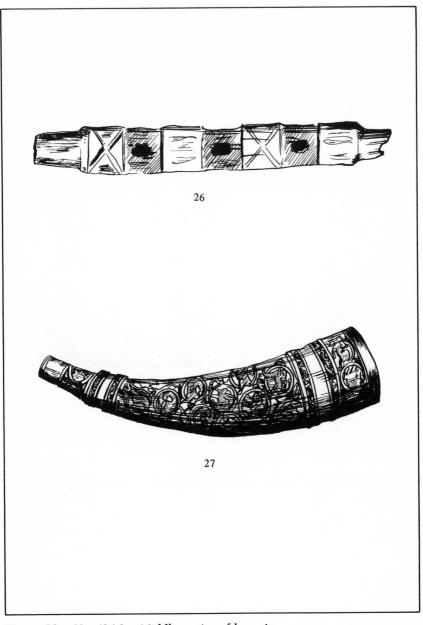

26

27

Figure 26.   *No. 434.2.*   Middle section of hornpipe.
Figure 27.   *No. 441.32.*   Classic oliphant, probably southern Italy, eleventh century.

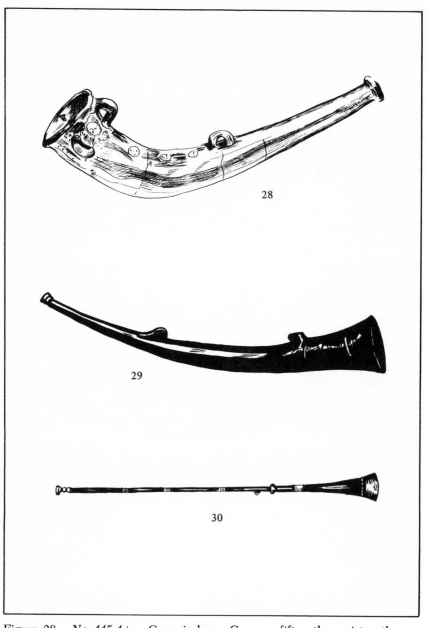

Figure 28. *No. 445.4+.* Ceramic horn, German, fifteenth or sixteenth century (?).

Figure 29. *No. 447.02.* Bronze or brass horn, thirteenth century (?).

Figure 30. *No. 449.2.* Buisine, seventeenth century (?).

BIBLIOGRAPHY

BIBLIOGRAPHY

Adcock, Ernest E. "Some Spanish Organs and Their Cases." *The Organ* 33 (1953–54):161–167, 3 pls.; 34 (1954–55):28–34, 3 pls.; corrections p. 49.

Åmark, Mats. *Sveriges medeltida kyrkklockor. Bevarade och kända klockor.* Stockholm: Almqvist & Wiksell, 1960.

Andersen, S. A. *Guldhornene fra Gallehus. Et par nye rekonstruktioner og deres forudsætninger.* (Populær-videnskabeligt Forlag, Studiesræde 3.) Copenhagen: Borgen, 1945.

Anderson, Harry. "Runeindskriften paa guldhornet fra Gallehus," *Sønderjydsk Maanedsskrift* 14 (1938):131–138.

Andersson, Otto. *The Bowed-Harp.* Translated and edited by Kathleen Schlesinger. London: William Reeves, 1930.

Anoyanakis, Fivos. "Ein byzantinisches Musikinstrument." *Acta musicologica* 37 (1965):158–165, 2 pls.

Arbatsky, Yury. "Baltikum." *Die Musik in Geschichte und Gegenwart* 1 (1949–51), cols. 1187–1194, Pl. 45.

Armstrong, Robert Bruce. *The Irish and the Highland Harps.* Edinburgh: David Douglas, 1904. Reprint. Shannon: Irish University Press, 1969; New York: Frederick Praeger, 1970.

Arro, Elmar. "Zum Problem der Kannel." *Sitzungsberichte der Gelehrten Estnischen Gesellschaft 1929* (Tartu, 1931):158–190, 5 pls.

Artsikhovsky, A. V., and Kolchin, B. A., eds. *Trudy Novgorodskoĭ arkheologicheskoĭ ekspeditsii.* (Akademiya Nauk SSSR. Institut Arkheologii. Materialy i issledovaniya po arkheologii SSSR, 55, 65, 117, 123.) Moscow: 1956–63.

Atlas van Nederland. The Hague: Staatsdrukkerij- en Uitgeverijbedrijf, 1960– .

Bachmann, Werner. *Die Anfänge des Streichinstrumentenspiels.* (Musikwissenschaftliche Einzeldarstellungen, 3.) Leipzig: Breitkopf & Härtel, 1964. English trans. by Norma Deane as *The Origins of Bowing.* London: Oxford University Press, 1969.

Baeksted, Anders. "The Stenmagle Rune Box and the Golden Horn Inscription." *Acta archaeologica* 18 (1947): 202–210.

Baines, Anthony. *Bagpipes.* (Pitt Rivers Museum, Occasional Papers on Technology, 9.) Oxford: Oxford University Press, 1960.

Baines, Anthony. *European and American Musical Instruments.* London: William Clowes and Sons; New York: Viking, 1966.

Barrett, J. H. "A Fipple Flute or Pipe from the Site of Keynsham Abbey." *The Galpin Society Journal* 22 (1969):47–50.

Bartha, Dénes. *A Jánoshidai avarkori kettőssíp* (*Die avarische Doppelschalmei von Jánoshida*). (Archaeologia Hungarica, 14.) Budapest: Magyar Történeti Múzeum, 1934.

Bate, Philip. *The Trumpet and Trombone.* London: Ernest Benn; New York: W. W. Norton, 1966.

Behn, Friedrich. "Eine antike Syrinx aus dem Rheinland." *Die Musik* 12, Part 2 (1912–13):285–286, plate.

Behn, Friedrich. *Musikleben im Altertum und frühen Mittelalter.* Stuttgart: Hiersemann, 1954.

Beigbeder, O. *Ivory.* New York: G. P. Putnam's Sons, 1965.

Bessaraboff, Nicholas. *Ancient European Musical Instruments.* Boston: Published for the Museum of Fine Arts, Boston, by the Harvard University Press, 1941. Reprint. New York: October House, 1964.

Bessinger, Jess. "*Beowulf* and the Harp at Sutton Hoo." *University of Toronto Quarterly* 27 (1957–58):148–168.

Bibby, Geoffry. *The Testimony of the Spade.* New York: Alfred A. Knopf, 1956.

Biddle, Martin, et al. "The Deserted Medieval Village of Seacourt, Berkshire." *Oxoniensia* 26/27 (1961–62): 70–201.

Boalch, Donald. *Makers of the Harpsichord and Clavichord, 1440 to 1840.* London: George Ronald, 1956.

Bock, Franz. "Über den Gebrauch der Hörner im altertum und das Vorkommen geschnitzer Elfenbeinhörner im Mittelalter." In Gustav Heider and Rudolph v. Eitelberger, eds., *Mittelalterliche Kunstdenkmale des Österreichischen Kaiserstaates.* 2 vols. Stuttgart: Ebner & Seubert, 1858–60. Vol. II, pp. 127ff.

Bock, Franz, and Willemsen, M. *Die mittlelalterliche Kunst- und Reliquienschätze zu Maestricht.* Cologne: 1872. French ed., enlarged, Maestricht, 1873.

Boeles, P. C. J. A. *Friesland tot de elfde eeuw.* 2d ed. The Hague: Martinus Nijhoff, 1951.

Bösken, Franz. "Historische Orgeln im Mainzer Raum." *Acta organologica* 3 (1969):69–87, Pl. 1, 9–11.

Bonanni, Filippo. *Gabinetto armonico pieno d'instromenti sonori . . . .* Rome: Giorgio Placho, 1723 (and other eighteenth- and nineteenth-century editions). The 152 engravings edited by Frank Ll. Harrison and Joan Rimmer as *The Showcase of Musical Instruments.* London: Constable; Toronto: McClelland and Stewart; New York: Dover, 1964.

Bouman, A. *De orgels in de Groote of Martinikerk te Groningen.* Amsterdam: H. J. Paris, 1941.

———. *Orgels in Nederland.* 2d ed. (Heemschutserie, no. 34.) Amsterdam: Allert de Lange, 1949.

Bragard, Roger, and De Hen, Ferdinand J. *Musical Instruments in Art and History.* London: Barrie & Rockliff, 1968. Also editions in Flemish, French, German, and Italian.

Braschowanov, Stojan. "Bulgarische Musik." *Die Musik in Geschichte und Gegenwart* 2 (1952): cols. 453–461, Pl. 16.

Braun, Hugh. "Bungay Castle. 1. Note on Excavations in 1936," *Proceedings of the Suffolk Institute of Archaeology and Natural History* 22 (1936).

Bridge, Joseph C. "Horns." *Journal of the Chester and North Wales Architectural, Archaeological and Historical Society,* n.s. 11 (1905):85–166, 12 pls.

Brix, Hans. *Guldhornene fra Gallehus. Med et tillæg om Gundestrup-Karret.* Copenhagen: Gyldendal, 1949.

Brøgger, Anton Wilhelm, Falk, H. J., and Schetelig, Haakon. *Osebergfundet.* 4 vols. Oslo: Universitetets Oldsaksamling, 1917–28. Volumes numbered I–III and V.

Brøndsted, Johannes. *Guldhornene. En oversigt.* Copenhagen: Nationalmuseet, 1954.

———. *Danmarks oldtid.* Vol. III, *Jernalderen.* Copenhagen: Gyldendal, 1960.

Broholm, H. C., Larsen, W. P., and Skjerne, G. *The Lures of the Bronze Age.* Copenhagen: Gyldendal, 1949.

Bruce-Mitford, R. L. S. "The Sutton Hoo Ship-Burial." *Proceedings of the Royal Institution of Great Britain* 34 (1947–50):440–449, 2 pls.

———. "The Sutton Hoo Ship-Burial." *Nature* 165 (1950):339–341.

Bruce-Mitford, Rupert and Myrtle. "The Sutton Hoo Lyre, *Beowulf,* and the Origins of the Frame Harp." *Antiquity* 44 (1970):7–13, Pls. I–VII.

Buchner, Alexander. *Musikinstrumente im Wandel der Zeiten.* Prague: Artia, 1956. Also Czech and English editions.

Buhle, Edward. *Die musikalischen Instrumente in den Miniaturen des frühen Miniaturen des frühen Mittelalters.* Vol. I, *Die Blasinstrumente, Leipzig:* Breitkopf & Härtel, 1903.

Bull, Edvard, et al. *Det norske folks liv og historie gjennem tidene.* 10 vols. Oslo: H. Aschenhoug, 1929–35.

Burchard, A. M. *A Guide to Weoley Castle.* Birmingham: City Museum and Art Gallery, 1965.

Burns, Joseph A. "The Organs of San Petronio, Bologna." *The Organ* 40 (1960–61):191–196.

Cahier, Charles. *Nouveaux mélanges d'archéologie, d'histoire et de littérature sur le Moyen âge.* Vol. II, *Ivoires, miniatures, émaux.* Paris: Firmin Didot, 1874.

Casey, D. A. "Lydney Castle." *Antiquaries Journal* 11 (1931):240–261, Pls. XXX–XXXVI.

Cellier, A. "L'orgue de la Cathédrale d'Embrun." *Bulletin de la Société d'études historiques, scientifiques, et littéraires des Hautes-Alpes,* no. 56 (1964): 102–106, 1 pl.

Cervelli, Luisa. *Contributi alla storia degli strumenti musicali in Italia/Rinascimento e barocco.* (Antiquae musicae italicae subsidia didascalica.) Bologna: Tamari, 1967.

Chouquet, Gustave. *Le musée du Conservatoire National de Musique. Catalogue descriptif et raisonné.* Nouvelle éd. Paris: Firmin Didot, 1884.

Closs, Adolf. "Notes on a Gothic signal horn recently acquired by the Zeughaus, Berlin." Zeitschrift für historische Waffen- und Kostümkunde, n.f. 3 (1931): 271–272.

Closson, Ernest. "L'olifant." *Revue musicale belge* 2 (1926):446–456, 1 pl.

Coles, J. M. "Irish Bronze Age Horns and Their Relations with Northern Europe." *Proceedings of the Prehistoric Society* 29 (1963):326–356, 2 pls.

Collaer, Paul, and Van der Linden, Albert. *Atlas historique de la musique.* Paris: Elsevier, 1960.

Cosma, Viorel. "Musikhistorisch interessante Funde bei Ausgrabungen in Rumänien." *Beiträge zur Musikwissenschaft* 7 (1965):153–154.

————. "Archäologische musikalische Funde in Rumänien." *Beiträge zur Musikwissenschaft* 8 (1966):3–14; Bildbeilage, pp. 89–96.

Dalton, O. M. "The Clephane Horn." *Archaeologia* 65 (1914):213–222, Pl. XXIV.

Darkevich, V. P. and Mongaĭt, A. L. "Staroryazanskiĭ klad 1966 goda." *Sovetskaya arkheologiya 1967,* Part 2:211–223, 2 pls.

Densmore, Frances. *Handbook of the Collection of Musical Instruments in the United States National Museum.* (Smithsonian Institution. U.S. National Museum. Bulletin 136.) Washington: U.S. Government Printing Office, 1927.

Disertori, Benvenuto. "Il più antico esemplare esistente di strumento ad arco." *Rivista musicale italiana* 42 (1938):294–308.

Dufourcq, Norbert, ed. *La musique des origines à nos jours.* Paris: Larousse, 1946.

————. *Le livre de l'orgue français 1589–1789.* Vol. II, *Le buffet.* (La vie musicale en France sous les rois Bourbons, 14.) Paris: A. and J. Picard, 1969.

Eberstaller, Oskar. *Orgeln und Orgelbauer in Österreich.* (Wiener musikwissenschaftliche Beiträge, 1.) Graz, and Cologne: Hermann Böhlaus Nachf., 1955.

Elliston-Erwood, Frank C. "Notes on Bronze Objects from Shooters Hill, Kent and Elsewhere and on the Antiquity of 'Jew's Harps'." *Archaeologia cantiana* 56 (1943):34–40.

————. "Further Notes of Jew's Harps." *Archaeologia cantiana* 60 (1947): 107–108.

Emsheimer, Ernst. "Die Streichleier von Danczk." *Svensk tidskrift for musikforskning* 43 (1961):109–117. Reprinted in Emsheimer, *Studia ethnomusicologica eurasiatica.* (Musikhistoriska Museets skrifter, 1.) Stockholm: Musikhistoriska Museet, 1964. Pp. 99–107.

————. "Lyra." *Kulturhistorisk leksikon for nordisk middelalder* 11 (Copenhagen: Rosenkilde og Bagger, 1966): cols. 21–23.

Engel, Carl. *A Descriptive Catalogue of the Musical Instruments in the South Kensington Museum.* London: Her Majesty's Stationery Office, 1874.

————. *Researches into the Early History of the Violin Family.* London: Novello, Ewer & Co.; Boston: Ditson, 1883.

"English Medieval Gittern." *British Museum Quarterly* 29 (1964–65):35–36.

Erici, Einar. *Inventarium över bevarade äldre kyrkorglar i Sverige tillkomna före mitten av 1800-talet . . . .* Stockholm: Kyrkomusikernas riksförbund, 1965.

Falke, Otto von. "Elfenbeinhörner. I. Ägypten und Italien. II. Byzanz." *Pantheon* 4 (1929):511–517; and 5 (1930):39–44.

Falke, Otto von, ed. *Die Sammlung Dr. Albert Figdor, Wien.* Part I, 5 vols. Vienna: Artaria, Glückselig; Berlin: Paul Cassirer, 1930.

Fallou, Robert, and Dufourcq, Norbert. *Essai d'une bibliographie de l'histoire de l'orgue en France*. Paris: Fischbacher, 1929.

Famintsyn, Aleksandr Sergeevich. *Gusli. Russkiĭ narodnyĭ muzykal'nyĭ instrument. Istoricheskiĭ ocherk*. St. Petersburg: Academy of Sciences, 1890.

Farmer, Henry George. *Islam*. (Musikgeschichte in Bildern, vol. 3, fasc. 2.) Leipzig: Deutscher Verlag für Musik, 1966.

Faussett, Bryan. *Inventorium sepulchrale*. London: T. Richards, 1856.

Fedorov, G. B. "Itogi trekhletnikh rabot v Moldavii v oblasti slavyano-russkoĭ arkheologii." *Akademiya Nauk SSSR. Institut istorii material'noĭ kul'tury. Kratkie soobshcheniya* 56 (1954):8–23, folding map.

Feicht, Hieronim. "Polen. I–IV." *Die Musik in Geschichte und Gegenwart* 10 (1962): cols. 1385–1400, Pl. 83.

Fleischer, Oskar. "Die Musikinstrumente des Altertums und Mittelalters in germanischen Ländern." In Hermann Paul, *Grundriss der germanischen Philologie* 3 (2d. ed. Strassburg: Karl J. Trübner, 1900). Pp. 567–576.

Folmer, A. "Alte Gerippe aus der Wierde von Lütje Saaxum." *Verhandlungen der Berliner Gesellschaft für Anthropologie, Ethnologie und Urgeschichte* 1878 (supplement to *Zeitschrift für Ethnologie* 10 (1878)):192–198.

Francis, E. B. "Rayleigh Castle: New Facts in its History and Recent Explorations on its Site." *Transactions of the Essex Archaeological Society*, n.s. 12 (1913):147–185, Pls. A–G.

Fremersdorf, Fritz. "Zwei wichtige Frankengräber aus Köln." *IPEK, Jahrbuch für prähistorische und ethnographische Kunst* 15/16 (1941–42):124–139, Pls. 48–57.

—————. "Ältestes Christentum, mit besonderer Berücksichtigung der Grabungsergebnisse unter der Severinskirche in Köln." *Kölner Jahrbuch für Vor- und Frühgeschichte* 2 (1956):7–26, Pls. 1–20.

Friedel, E. *Verhandlungen der Berliner Gesellschaft für Anthropologie, Ethnologie und Urgeschichte* 1876 (supplement to *Zeitschrift für Ethnologie* 8 (1876)):45–47, Pl. VIII. (Report on several excavated objects.)

Gale, Samuel. "An Historical Dissertation upon the antient Danish Horn, kept in the Cathedral Church of York." *Archaeologia* 1 (3d ed., 1804):187–202, 202*.

Galpin, Francis W. *Old English Instruments of Music*. Chicago: A. C. McClurg; London: Methuen, 1911; 4th ed., revised, with supplementary notes by Thurston Dart. New York: Barnes & Noble, 1965.

Gass, J. *Les orgues de la Cathédrale de Strasbourg à travers les siècles*. Strasbourg, 1935.

Gastoué, Amédée. *L'orgue en France de l'antiquité au début de la période classique*. Paris: La "Schola," 1921.

Gay, Victor. *Glossaire archéologique du Moyen âge et de la Renaissance*. 2 vols. Paris: Société Bibliographique, 1887, and Auguste Picard, 1928. Reprint. Nendeln, Liechtenstein: Kraus Reprint, 1967.

Geiringer, Karl. *Musical Instruments*. London: Oxford University Press, 1943; New York: Oxford University Press, 1945.

Gensoles, l'Abbé. *France. Comité historique des Arts et Monuments. Bulletin archéologique* 3 (1844–45):176–177. (Note on the organ of Soliès-Ville and its inscription.)

Gessler, E. A. "Die Harschhörner der Innerschweizer." *Anzeiger für schweizerische Altertumskunde*, n.f. 27 (1925):27–40, 83–94, 168–181, 228–250.

Glück, Heinrich, and Dietz, Ernst. *Die Kunst des Islam*. Berlin: Propyläen-Verlag, 1925.

Goldron, Romain. *Byzantine and Medieval Music*. In *History of Music*, edited by Romain Goldron, vol. 2. New York: H. S. Stuttman, 1968.

Goldschmidt, Adolph. *Die Elfenbeinskulpturen*. 4 vols. (Denkmäler der deutschen Kunst.) Berlin: Bruno Cassirer, 1914–26.

Green, Charles. *Sutton Hoo*. London: Merlin Press; New York: Barnes & Noble, 1963.

Grove, L. R. A. "Archaeological Notes from Maidstone Museum." *Archaeologia cantiana* 69 (1955):206–215.

————. "Archaeological Notes from Maidstone Museum." *Archaeologia cantiana* 70 (1956):268–273.

Grundmann, Günther, ed. *Deutscher Glockenatlas*. Vol. I. *Württemberg und Hohenzollern*. Munich: Deutscher Kunstverlag, 1959.

Gustafson, Gabriel. *Norges oldtid. Mindesmaerker og oldsager*. (Gammel norsk kultur i tekst og billeder.) Oslo: Alb. Cammermeyer, 1906.

Haacke, Walter. *Orgeln in aller Welt. Organs of the World. Orgues du monde entier*. (Die blauen Bücher.) Königstein im Taunus: Karl Robert Langewiesche Nachfolger Hans Köster, 1965; London: George Allen & Unwin, 1966.

Hammerstein, Reinhold. "Instrumenta Hieronymi." *Archiv für Musikwissenschaft* 16 (1959):117–134, 4 pls.

"The Harp that Never . . . and the Lyre that Once." *The British Museum Society Bulletin*, no. 3 (February 1970):8–9.

Harrison, Frank Ll., and Rimmer, Joan. *European Musical Instruments*. London: Studio Vista; New York: W. W. Norton, 1964.

Hartner, Willy. *Die Goldhörner von Gallehus*. Wiesbaden: Franz Steiner, 1969.

d'Haucourt, Geneviève. "Comment se divertissait-on au Moyen âge?" *Archaeologia*, no. 8 (January-February, 1966):65–68.

Hayward, Richard. *The Story of the Irish Harp*. London: Arthur Guiness, 1954.

Hefner [-Alteneck], Jakob Heinrich von, and Wolf, Johann Wilhelm. *Die Burg Tannenberg und ihre Ausgrabungen*. Frankfurt a. M.: S. Schmerber'sche Buchhandlung (Nachfolger H. Keller), 1850.

Hefner-Alteneck, Jakob Heinrich von. *Trachten, Kunstwerke und Geräthschaften vom frühen Mittelalter bis ende des achtzehnten Jahrhunderts nach gleichzeitigen Originalen*. 2d ed., 10 vols. Frankfurt a. M.: Heinrich Keller, 1879–89.

Hennerberg, C. F. "Die schwedischen Orgeln des Mittelalters." In *III. Kongress der Internationalen Musikgesellschaft Wien . . . 1909*. Vienna: Artaria; Leipzig: Breitkopf & Härtel, 1909. Pp. 91–99.

————. "Orglar i norden under medeltiden." In *Musik och musikinstrument,* ed. Otto Andersson. Nordisk Kultur, 25. Stockholm, Oslo, Copenhagen, 1934. Pp. 70–80.

Hickmann, Hans. *Instruments de musique.* (Catalogue général des antiquités du Musée du Caire, nos. 69.201–69.852.) Cairo: Imprimerie de l'Institut Français d'Archéologie Orientale, 1949.

Hill, Arthur George. "The Medieval Organs at Lübeck, and Some Other Ancient Organs." *Archaeologia* 51 (1888):419–426, Pls. XV-XVII.

———. "Mediaeval Organs in Spain." *Sammelbände der Internationalen Musikgesellschaft* 14 (1912–13):487–490.

———. *The Organ-Cases and Organs of the Middle Ages and Renaissance.* (Bibliotheca Organologica, 6.) Hilversum: Frits Knuf, 1966. (Reprint in one volume of the two-volume edition. London: David Bogue, 1883, and Charles Whittingham, 1891.)

Hipkins, Alfred J. *Musical Instruments Historic, Rare and Unique.* Edinburgh: A. and C. Black, 1888. Reprint. London: A. and C. Black, 1921.

Hirt, Franz Josef. *Meisterwerke des Klavierbaus.* Olten: Urs Graf-Verlag, 1955.

Hołubowicz, Włodzimierz. "Wczesnośredniowieczne instrumenty muzyczne z badań w Opolu." *Ruch muzyczny,* no. 19 (Cracow, 1958):33.

Hołubowicz, Włodzimierz, and L. Pietkiewicz. "Skrzypce polskie z XI w. z badań w Opolu." *Archeologia śląska* 2 (1959):191–198, and Pl. VIII.

Hornbostel, Erich M. von, and Sachs, Curt. "Systematik der Musikinstrumente." *Zeitschrift für Ethnologie* 46 (1914):553–590. Translation by Anthony Baines and Klaus P. Wachsmann. *The Galpin Society Journal* 14 (1961):3–29.

Hume, Abraham. *Ancient Meols.* London: John Russell Smith, 1863.

Hunt, Edgar. *The Recorder and its Music.* London: H. Jenkins, 1962; New York: W. W. Norton, 1963.

Huyghe, René, ed. *Larousse Encyclopedia of Byzantine and Medieval Art.* New York: Prometheus Press, 1963.

Jankuhn, H. *Die Ausgrabungen in Haithabu 1937–1939.* Deutsche Ahnenerbe, vol. 3. Berlin: Ahnenerbe-Stiftung, 1943.

Jażdżewski, Konrad. "Kilka uzupełniających uwag o gęślach gdańskich." *Z otchłani wieków* 19 (1950–51):102–104.

———. "Najstarsze zachowane gęśle słowiańskie." *Z otchłani wieków* 19 (1950–51):13–18.

———. "Uwagi dodatkowa o gęślach gdańskich." *Z otchłani wieków* 20 (1951):99–101.

———. "O zagadnieniu polskich instrumentów strunowych z wczesnego średniowiecza." *Prace i materiały Muzeum Archeologicznego i Etnograficznego w Łodzi, Seria archeologiczna* 12 (1966):7–35.

Jewitt, Llewellyn. "The Burghmote Horns and the Office of Horn-blower." *The Antiquary* 1 (1880):252–256.

Jones, E. Alfred. "The Drinking Horns and Silver Plate in the National Museum at Copenhagen." *Burlington Magazine* 15 (1909):221–232.

Kamiński, Włodzimierz. "Frühmittelalterliche Musikinstrumente auf polnischem Gebiet." In *The Book of the First International Musicological Congress*

Devoted to the Works of Frederick Chopin, edited by Zofia Lissa. Warsaw: PWN–Polish Scientific Publishers, 1963. Pp. 551–558.

―――. "Beiträge zur Erforschung der frühmittelalterlichen Musikinstrumente der Nordwest- und Ostslawen." In *Anfänge der slavischen Musik.* Bratislava: Vydavateľstvo Slovenskej akadémie vied, 1966. Pp. 139–146.

―――. "Instrumentarium muzyczne w Polsce średniowiecznej." *Musica medii aevi* 2 (1968):7–39.

Karstädt, Georg. "Horninstrumente. C. Mittelalter und Neuzeit." *Die Musik in Geschichte und Gegenwart* 6 (1957):cols. 744–756, Pls. 31–33.

―――. "Lübeck." *Die Musik in Geschichte und Gegenwart* 8 (1960): cols. 1266–1279, Pls. 62–63.

―――. *Lasst lustig die Hörner erschallen! Eine kleine Kulturgeschichte der Jagdmusik.* Hamburg and Berlin: Paul Parey, 1964.

Kendrick, T. D. "The Horn of Ulph." *Antiquity* 11 (1937):278–282, 5 pl.

Kiersnowska, T. "Gwizdek z grodziska wcesnośredniowiecznego w Bródnie Starym pow. Warszawski." *Sprawozdania P. M. A.* (Warsaw, 1951):107–109.

Kinsky, Georg. *Musikhistorisches Museum von Wilhelm Heyer in Cöln. Katalog.* Vol. II, *Zupf- und Streichinstrumente.* Cologne: Wilhelm Heyer, 1912.

―――. *Geschichte der Musik in Bildern.* Leipzig: Breitkopf & Härtel, 1929.

Kjellberg, Sven T. "Mungigan." *Kulturen 1947* (Lund, 1948):24–25.

Klier, Karl M. *Volkstümliche Musikinstrumente in den Alpen.* Kassel: Bärenreiter, 1956.

Klotz, Hans. "Orgel. IV. Die Kirchenorgel bis um 1500." *Die Musik in Geschichte und Gegenwart* 10 (1962): cols. 266–272.

Knowles, William James. "Portion of a Harp and Other Objects Found in the Crannoge of Carncoagh, Co. Antrim." *Journal of the Royal Society of Antiquaries of Ireland* 27 (1897):114–115.

Koechlin, Raymond. *Les ivoires gothiques français.* 3 vols. Paris: Auguste Picard, 1924.

Kolchin, Boris Aleksandrovich. "K itogam rabot Novgorodskoĭ arkheologicheskoĭ ekspeditsii (1951–1962 gg.)." *Akademiya Nauk SSSR. Institut Arkheologii. Kratkie soobshcheniya* 99 (1964):3–20.

―――. *Novgorodskie drevnosti. Derevyannye izdeliya.* (Akademiya Nauk SSSR. Institut Arkheologii. Arkheologiya SSSR. Svod arkheologicheskikh istochnikov, E1–55.) Moscow: Izdateľstvo "Nauka," 1968.

Krautwurst, Franz. "Konrad Paumann in Nördlingen." In *Festschrift Heinrich Besseler zum sechzigsten Geburtstag.* Leipzig: Deutscher Verlag für Musik, 1961. Pp. 203–210.

―――. "Das Wirken des Breslauer Orgelbauers Stephan Kaschendorff in Nördlingen 1466–1483." *Jahrbuch für fränkische Landesforschung* 24 (1964):145–165.

Van 'T Kruijs, Marinus H. *Verzameling van disposities der verschillende orgels in Nederland* . . . . Rotterdam: Corns. Immig, 1885. Reprint. Amsterdam: Frits A. M. Knuf, 1962.

Kühnel, Ernst. "Die sarazenischen Olifanthörner." *Jahrbuch der Berliner Museen* 1 (1959):33–50.

————. "Ivory in the East. *Islam.*" *Encyclopedia of World Art* 8 (New York: McGraw-Hill, 1963): cols. 772–777. Also Italian ed.

Kunz, George Frederick. *Ivory and the Elephant in Art, in Archaeology, and in Science.* Garden City, and New York: Doubleday, Page, 1916.

Lacroix, Paul. *Manners, Customs, and Dress During the Middle Ages and During the Renaissance Period.* London: Chapman and Hall, 1874. Translated from *Moeurs, usages et costumes du Moyen Age et à l'époque de la Renaissance.* Paris: Firmin Didot, 1871.

Land, J. P. N. "Twee aloude fluiten, in Nederland opgegraven." *Tijdschrift der Vereeniging voor Noord-Nederlands Muziekgeschiedenis* 4 (1894):33–35.

Langwill, Lyndesay G. *An Index of Musical Wind-Instrument Makers.* Edinburgh: Privately printed, 1960.

————. Review of Baines (1960). *Notes* 19 (1961–62):65–66.

Larousse de la musique. 2 vols. Paris: Larousse, 1957.

Löw, Giuseppe. "Crepitacolo." *Enciclopedia cattolica* 4 (Vatican City, 1950): cols. 846–847.

Longhurst, Margaret Helen. *Victoria and Albert Museum. Department of Architecture and Sculpture. Catalogue of Carvings in Ivory.* 2 vols. London: Board of Education, 1927, 1929.

————. "An Eleventh-Century Oliphant." *Burlington Magazine* 62 (1933): 194–195.

Lütgendorff, Willibald Leo Frh. von. *Die Geigen- und Lautenmacher vom Mittelalter bis zur Gegenwart.* Frankfurt a. M.: H. Keller, 1904. 5th and 6th ed. 2 vols. Frankfurt a. M., and Berlin: Frankfurter Verlags-Anstalt, 1922.

Lunelli, Renato. *Die Orgelwerke von S. Petronio in Bologna.* (Orgel-Monographien, 13.) Mainz: Rheingold-Verlag, 1956.

————. "Vecchi organi scomparsi dalle chiese di Trento." *L'organo* 5 (1967): 159–174, 1 pl.

Marcuse, Sibyl. *Musical Instruments at Yale.* New Haven: Yale University Art Gallery, 1960.

————. *Musical Instruments: A Comprehensive Dictionary.* Garden City, N.Y.: Doubleday, 1964.

Marigold, W. G. "Observations on German Organ Cases." *The Organ* 42 (1962–63):80–85.

Marković, Maja and Zvonimir. "Dvostruka sviraljka iz bjelo-brdske avarsko-slavenske nekropole VII–IX st." *Muzička revija* 2 (Zagreb, 1951):36–41.

Maskell, Alfred. *Ivories.* New York: G. P. Putnam's Sons; London: Methuen, 1905. Reprint. Rutland, Vt.: Charles E. Tuttle, 1966.

Meaney, Audrey. *A Gazetteer of Early Anglo-Saxon Burial Sites.* London: George Allen & Unwin, 1964.

Megaw, J. V. S. "Penny Whistles and Prehistory." *Antiquity* 34 (1960):6–13, Pl. II.

————. "An End-Blown Flute or Flageolet from White Castle." *Medieval Archaeology* 5 (1961):176–180, Pl. XXIX.

————. "A Medieval Bone Pipe from White Castle, Monmouthshire." *The Galpin Society Journal* 16 (1963):85–94, Pl. 8–9; 17 (1964):116–117.

————. "The Earliest Musical Instruments in Europe." *Archaeology* 21 (1968):124–132.

————. "An End-Blown Flute from Medieval Canterbury." *Medieval Archaeology* 12 (1968):149–150, Pl. XXIII.

————. "Problems and Non-Problems in Palaeo-Organology: a Musical Miscellany." In *Studies in Ancient Europe. Essays Presented to Stuart Piggott.* Leicester: Leicester University Press, 1968. Pp. 333–358, Pls. XIV–XVI.

Milliken, William Mathewson. "The Acquisition of Six Objects from the Guelph Treasure for the Cleveland Museum of Art." *Bulletin of the Cleveland Museum of Art* 17 (1930):165–177.

Mischiati, Oscar, and Tagliavini, Luigi Ferdinando. "La situazione degli antichi organi in Italia. Problemi di censimento e di tutela." *L'Organo* 7 (1969):3–61, 8 pls.

Mitrea, Bucur. "Un instrument muzical din perioada feudală timpurie descoperit la Bisericuţa-Garvăn." *Academia Republicii populare romîne. Institutul de arheologie. Studii şi cercetări de istorie veche* 13 (1962):197–200.

Moeck, Hermann Alexander. "Die skandinavischen Kernspaltflöten in Vorzeit und Tradition der Folklore." *Svensk tidskrift for musikforskning* 36 (1954): 56–83.

Moeck, Hermann. *Typen europäischer Blockflöten in Vorzeit, Geschichte und Volksüberlieferung.* Celle: Privately printed, 1967.

————. "Typen europäischer Kernspaltflöten." In *Studia instrumentorum musicae popularis* 1, Erich Stockmann, ed. (Musikhistoriska Museets skrifter, 3.) Stockholm: Musikhistoriska Museet, 1969. Pp. 41–73, 7 pls. (The contents are nearly identical to those of Moeck (1967), and for this reason, the present catalogue makes reference only to the latter.)

Molinier, Émile. *Histoire générale des arts appliqués à l'industrie du Ve à la fin du XVIIIe siècle.* Vol. I, *Ivoires.* Paris: E. Levy, 1896.

————. *Musée national du Louvre. Département des objets d'art du Moyen âge, de la Renaissance et des temps modernes. Catalogue des ivoires.* Paris: Librairies-Imprimeries Réunies, 1896.

————. "Quelques ivoires récemment acquis par le Louvre." *Gazette des Beaux-Arts,* Troisième Période, 20 (1898):481–493.

Münger, F. "Die gotische Orgel in der Valeria-Kirche in Sitten." *Musik und Gottesdienst* 9 (1955).

Nielsen, S. Vestergaard. "Blokfløjter fra oldtid og middelalder; en nyfunden jernalderfløjte fra Vesthimmerland." *Kuml* 1 (1951):145–153.

Niemeyer, Wilhelm. "Awarische Musik." *Die Musik in Geschichte und Gegenwart* 1 (1949–51): cols. 899–900.

————. "Flöteninstrumente. D. Vor- und Frühgeschichte: Europa." *Die Musik in Geschichte und Gegenwart* 4 (1955): cols. 330–335.

————. "Germanische Musik." *Die Musik in Geschichte und Gegenwart* 4 (1955): cols. 1809–1819, Pls. 74–76.

Norlind, Tobias. *Systematik der Saiteninstrumente.* Vol. I, *Geschichte der Zither.* Stockholm: Fritzes K. Hofbuchhandlung, 1936. Vol. II, *Geschichte des Klaviers.* Hannover: Albert Küster, 1939.

_____. *Musikinstrumentens historia i ord och bild*. Stockholm: Nordisk Rotogravyr, 1941.

Oldeberg, Andreas. "Vallhorn, herdepipor och lurar." *Värmland förr och nu* 48 (1950):19–67.

_____. "Vorgeschichtliche Blashörner." *Musica* 6 (1952):149–152.

Ott, Alfons. *Ausstellung Alte Musik. Instrumente, Noten und Dokumente aus drei Jahrhunderten. Katalog*. Munich: Max Hieber, 1951.

Owart, Werner. "Die Orgel in der ehemaligen Benediktiner-Abteikirche zu Ossiach in Kärnten." *Carinthia I* 153, no. 1 (Klagenfurt, 1963):519–534.

Oxenstierna, Eric. "Die Goldhörner von Gallehus." *Forschungen und Fortschritte* 27 (1953):19–23.

_____. *Die Goldhörner von Gallehus*. Lidingö, Sweden: Privately printed, 1956.

Palošija, Đurđica. "Ranosredovječne panonske dvojne sviraljke." *Etnološki pregled* 2 (1960):63–84.

Panum, Hortense. "Harfe und Lyra im alten Nordeuropa." *Sammelbände der Internationalen Musikgesellschaft* 7 (1905–6):1–40.

_____. *Middelalderens strengeinstrumenter og deres forløbere i oldtiden*. 3 vols. Copenhagen: Lehmann & Stages Boghandel, 1915; P. Haase & Søns, 1928, 1931.

_____. *The Stringed Instruments of the Middle Ages*. Rev. and ed. by Jeffrey Pulver. London: William Reeves [1941]. Reprint. Westport, Conn.: Greenwood Press [1970].

Peate, Iorwerth C. "Welsh Musical Instruments." *Man* 47 (1947):21–25, Pl. B.

Pegge, et al. *Archaeologia* 3 (1786):1–34, Pls. I–VII. (Nine short articles on horns, the Welsh crwth and pibcorn.)

Petersen, Jan. "Paa rangel. Smaa studier i museene." In *Haakon Schetelig paa 40-aars dagen* . . . . Oslo, 1917. Pp. 35–40.

Pierquin de Gembloux, Claude-Charles. *Lettre à M. Bottée de Toulmon sur l'histoire de la guimbarde*. Bourges: Imprimerie de Manceron [1840].

Pierre, Joseph. "Une guimbarde antique." *Revue du Berry et du Centre* 61 (1935):101–105; 62 (1936):6–11.

Pitt-Rivers, Augustus H. L. F. "Excavations at Caesar's Camp near Folkestone, Conducted in June and July, 1878." *Archaeologia* 47 (1883):429–465, Pls. XVI–XX.

Pleyte, Willem. *De nederlandsche oudheden. Friesland-Oostergo*. Leiden: E. J. Brill, 1877.

Quoika, Rudolf. *Vom Blockwerk zur Registerorgel. Zur Geschichte der Orgelgotik, 1200–1520*. Kassel: Bärenreiter, 1966.

Raugel, Felix. *Les orgues et les organistes de la Cathédrale de Strasbourg*. Colmar: Éditions Alsatia, 1948.

Rautioaho, Asko. "Orgel." *Kulturhistorisk leksikon for nordisk middelalder* 12 (Copenhagen: Rosenkilde & Bagger, 1967): cols. 692–697.

Reinhard, Kurt. "Mandola, Mandora." *Die Musik in Geschichte und Gegenwart* 8 (1960): cols. 1571–1572, Pl. 82.

Remnant, Mary. "The Gittern in English Medieval Art." *The Galpin Society Journal* 18 (1965):104–109, Pls. 11–12.

Rensch, Roslyn. *The Harp. Its History, Technique and Repertoire.* London: Gerald Duckworth, 1969.

Reuter, Rudolf. *Orgeln in Westfalen. Inventar historischer Orgeln in Westfalen und Lippe.* Kassel: Bärenreiter, 1965.

Rice, David Talbot, ed. *The Dawn of European Civilization: The Dark Ages.* London: Thames and Hudson; New York: McGraw-Hill, 1965.

———. *Islamic Art.* New York, and Washington: Frederick A. Praeger; London: Thames and Hudson, 1965.

Richardson, Katherine M. "Excavations in Hungate, York." *Archaeological Journal* 116 (1959):51–114, folding figs., Pls. IV–VII.

Richter, Gerhard. "Eine Maultrommel aus Stendal." *Altmärkisches Museum Stendahl. Jahresgabe* 11 (1957):47–49, three photos.

Riedel, Friedrich Wilhelm. "Klavier. I–V." *Die Musik in Geschichte und Gegenwart* 7 (1958): cols. 1090–1101.

Riemsdijk, J. C. M. van. "Het orgel van de Nicolaïkerk te Utrecht." *Tijdschrift der Vereeniging voor Noord-Nederlands Muziekgeschiedenis* 2 (1887):195–199, folding pl.

Rimmer, Joan. "The Morphology of the Irish Harp." *The Galpin Society Journal* 17 (1964):39–49, Pls. V–VII.

Ringbom, Lars Ivar. "Gallenhushornens bilder." *Åbo, Akademi. Acta academiae aboensis. Humaniora* 18 (1949):258–304.

Roes, Anna. *Bone and Antler Objects from the Frisian Terp-Mounds.* Haarlem: H. D. Tjeenk Willink & Zoon, 1963.

———. *Vondsten van Dorestad.* (Archaeologica Traiectina, 7.) Groningen: J. B. Wolters, 1965.

Ruth-Sommer, Hermann. *Alte Musikinstrumente.* (Bibliothek für Kunst- und Antiquitätensammler, 8.) 2d ed. Berlin: Richard Carl Schmidt, 1920.

Rydbeck, Monica. "Maultrommeln in Funden aus dem schwedischen Mittelalter." In *Res medievales. Ragnar Blomqvist Kal. Mai. MCMLXVIII oblata.* (Archaeologica Lundensia, 3.) Lund: Kulturhistoriska museet, 1968. Pp. 252–261.

Rydbeck, Otto. *Den medeltida borgen i Skanör.* (Skrifter utgivna av Kungl. humanistika vetenskapssamfundet i Lund, 20.) Lund: C. W. K. Gleerup, 1935.

Rygh, Oluf. *Norske oldsager.* Oslo: Alb. Cammermeyer, 1885.

Sachs, Curt. *Handbuch der Musikinstrumentenkunde.* (Kleine Handbücher der Musikgeschichte nach Gattungen, 12.) Leipzig: Breitkopf & Härtel, 1930.

———. *The History of Musical Instruments.* New York: W. W. Norton, 1940.

Salmen, Walter. "Volksinstrumente in Westfalen." *Studia musicologica* 3 (1962):271–279.

"A Saxon Minstrel's Harp: Sutton Hoo Remains Reconstructed." *Illustrated London News* 212 (March 6, 1948):272.

Schiørring, Nils. "Dänemark." *Die Musik in Geschichte und Gegenwart* 2 (1952): cols. 1841–1857, Pls. 62–63.

Schlosser, Julius. *Die Sammlung alter Musikinstrumente. Beschreibendes Verzeichnis.* Vienna: Anton Schroll, 1920.

―――. *Unsere Musikinstrumente. Eine Einführung in ihre Geschichte.* Vienna: Anton Schroll, 1922.

Schnitzler, Hermann, Volbach, Fritz, and Bloch, Peter. *Skulpturen: Elfenbein. Perlmutter. Stein. Holz. Europäisches Mittelalter. Sammlung E. und M. Kofler-Truniger, Luzern.* Vol. I. Lucerne, and Stuttgart: Räber, 1964.

Schwarz, Joseph. "Aachen- oder Wetterhörner." *Geschichts- und Heimatblätter für das alte Herzogtum Jülich: "Das Rurland"* (June 2, 1935).

Scott, Walter. *The Border Antiquities of England and Scotland* . . . . 2 vols. London: 1814, 1817.

Servières, Georges. "La décoration des buffets d'orgue au XVe et XVIe siècles." *Gazette des Beaux-Arts* Période 4, vol. 12 (1916):457–473; Période 4, vol. 13 (1917):95–107.

Sevåg, Reidar. "Lur." *Kulturhistorisk leksikon for nordisk middelalder* 11 (Copenhagen: Rosenkilde & Bagger, 1966): cols. 9–11.

―――. "Die Spaltflöten Norwegens." In Erich Stockmann, ed., *Studia instrumentorum musicae popularis* 1 (Musikhistoriska Museets skrifter, 3.) Stockholm: Musikhistoriska Museet, 1969. Pp. 74–81, 4 pls.

Shetelig, Haakon, and Johannessen, F. *Kvalsundfundet og andre norske myrfund av fartøier.* (Skrifter Bergens Museums, N. r. B. II, Nr. 2.) Bergen, 1929.

Shewring, Walter. "Early Organs in North Germany." *The Organ* 39 (1959–60):109–118, 2 pls.

Simon, Alicja. "Na drozde historycznego rozwoju gęśli słowiańskich." In *Księga pamiątkowa ku czci prof. A. Chybińskiego.* Cracow, 1950. Pp. 347–353.

―――. "An Early Medieval Slav *Gesle.*" *The Galpin Society Journal* 10 (1957):63–65, 1 pl.

Skinner, William, et al. *The Belle Skinner Collection of Old Musical Instruments. Holyoke, Massachusetts.* Published by Wm. Skinner, 1933.

Skjerne, Godtfred, ed. *Carl Claudius' samling af gamle musikinstrumenter.* Copenhagen: Levin & Munksgaard, 1931.

―――. "Om guldhornene." *Musikhistorisk arkiv* 1 (1931–39):286–345.

Skov, Sigvard. "En mundgige fundet i Kolding." *Vejle amts aarbog* (1957): 25–28.

Smets, Paul. *Die berühmten Orgelwerke der Stadt Lübeck.* (Orgel-Monographien, 11.) Mainz: Rheingold-Verlag, 1945.

―――. *Die Orgel der St. Valentinuskirche zu Kiedrich.* (Orgel-Monographien, 6.) Mainz: Rheingold-Verlag, 1945.

Smoldon, William Lawrence. *A History of Music.* London: Herbert Jenkins, 1965.

Stahl, Wilhelm. *Die Totentanz-Orgel der Marienkirche zu Lübeck.* (Orgel-Monographien, 1.) Mainz: Paul Smets, 1932. 2d rev. ed. Mainz: Rheingold Verlag, 1942.

Stanley, Albert A. *Catalogue of the Stearns Collection of Musical Instruments.* Ann Arbor: University of Michigan, 1918.

Steger, Hugo. *David rex et propheta.* (Erlanger Beiträge zur Sprach- und Kunstwissenschaft, 6.) Nürnberg: Hans Carl, 1961.

Still, Barry C. "The Organ in the Church of St. Valentin, Kiedrich." *The Organ* 30 (1950–51):66–70, 1 pl.

Stone, Peter. "Some Famous Drinking-Horns in Britain." *Apollo* 74 (1961): 102–104, 143–145.

Strumiłło, T. "Jeszcze o gęślach gdańskich." *Z otchłani wieków* 20 (1951): 94–98.

Swarzenski, Hanns. "Two Oliphants in the Museum." *Boston Museum Bulletin* 60 (1962):27–45.

Tardy. *Les ivoires.* Paris: Tardy, 1966.

Teichmann, Eduard. "Zur Deutung der Worte 'dein eyn' auf dem Tragbande des sogenannten Karlshornes." *Aachener Geschichtsverein Zeitschrift* 25 (1903):1–27.

Thomas, Edit B. *Archäologische Funde in Ungarn.* Budapest: Corvina, 1956.

Thompson, Michael Welman. *Novgorod the Great: Excavations in the Medieval City 1951–62.* London: Evelyn, Adams & Mackay; New York: Frederick A. Praeger, 1967.

"A Tribute to Mr. Whittall." *The Consort,* no. 6 (1949):21–22, 1 pl.

Väisänen, Armas Otto, et al. "Kantele." *Kulturhistorisk leksikon for nordisk middelalder* 8 (Copenhagen: Rosenkilde & Bagger, 1963): cols. 243–245.

Vainer, I. S., and Nigomedzyanov, M. N. "Muzykal'nyĭ dukhovoĭ instrument iz Novogo Saraya." *Sovetskaya arkheologiya 1965,* Part 2:282–283.

van der Meer, John Henry. "Typologie der Sackpfeife." *Anzeiger des Germanischen Nationalmuseums 1964* (Nürnberg, 1964): 123–146.

Veeck, Walther. *Die Alamannen in Württemberg.* (Germanische Denkmäler der Völkerwanderungszeit, 1.) 2 vols. Berlin and Leipzig: Walter de Gruyter, 1931.

Vellekoop, Gerrit. "Voorlopers van onze blokfluiten." *Tijdschrift der Vereeniging voor Nederlandsche Muziekgeschiedenis* 20, no. 3 (1966):178–185, 1 pl.

Vente, Maarten A. *Die Brabanter Orgel. Zur Geschichte der Orgelkunst in Belgien und Holland im Zeitalter der Gotik und der Renaissance.* Amsterdam: H. J. Paris, 1958.

Vente, Maarten A., and Kok, W. "Organs in Spain and Portugal." *The Organ* 34 (1954–55):193–199, 3 pl.; 35 (1955–56):155–164, 3 pl., 203–212, 2 pl.; 37 (1957–58):37–43, 1 pl.

Vertkov, K., et al. *Atlas muzykal'nykh instrumentov narodov SSSR.* Moscow: Gosudarstvennoe Muzykal'noe Izdatel'stvo, 1963.

Viollet-le-Duc, Eugène. "Buffet (d'orgues)." *Dictionnaire raisonné de l'architecture française du XIe au XVIe siècle* 2 (Paris: Ve A. Morel, 1874):252–256.

Virchow, Rudolf. *Verhandlungen der Berliner Gesellschaft für Anthropologie, Ethnologie und Urgeschichte* 1873 (supplement to *Zeitschrift für Ethnologie*

5 (1873)). Pp. 189–192. (Report on "einen Torfschädel und zwei alte Knochenpfeifen aus Neu-Brandenburg.")

Volbach, W. F. *Staatliche Museen zu Berlin. Die Bildwerke des Deutschen Museums.* Vol. I, *Die Elfenbeinbildwerke.* Berlin and Leipzig: Walter de Gruyter, 1923.

Waring, J. B., ed., and Bedford, F., lithographer. *Art Treasures of the United Kingdom.* London, 1858.

Waterman, Dudley M. "Late Saxon, Viking, and Early Medieval Finds from York." *Archaeologia* 97 (1959):59–105, Pls. XVI–XXII.

Watts, W. W. "An English Horn with Fourteenth-Century Mounts." *Burlington Magazine* 52 (1928):277–278.

Werner, Joachim. "Leier und Harfe im germanischen Frühmittelalter." In *Aus Verfassungs- und Landesgeschichte. Festschrift für Theodor Mayer* 1. Constance, 1954. Pp. 9–15, 2 pls.

Wester, Bertil. *Gotisk resning i svenska orglar.* Stockholm: Generalstabens litografiska anstalt, 1936.

Wieczorowski, Tadeusz. "Wczesnohistoryczne instrumenty muzyczne kultury staropolskiej z Wielkopolski i Pomorza." *Wiadomości archeologiczne* 16 (1939):348–356, Pl. LXVI. Reprinted, 1948.

Williams, Peter. *The European Organ 1450–1850.* London: B. T. Batsford, 1966.

Williamson, George C. *The Book of Ivory.* London: Frederick Muller, 1938.

Winternitz, Emanuel. *Musical Instruments of the Western World.* London: Thames and Hudson; New York: McGraw-Hill, 1967. Translated by Werner Bachmann as *Die schönsten Musikinstrumente des Abendlandes.* Munich: Keysersche Verlagsbuchhandlung, 1966.

Witte, J. F. "Iets over het orgel in Nicolaïkerk te Utrecht." *Bouwsteenen* 3 (1874–81):92–100.

Wörsching, Joseph. *Die grosse Orgel der Kathedrale zu Reims.* (Orgel-Monographien, 15.) Mainz: Rheingold-Verlag, 1946.

———. *Die Orgelwerke des Münsters zu Strassburg i. E.* (Orgel-Monographien, 21.) Mainz: Rheingold-Verlag, 1947.

Worm, Ole. *Danicorum monumentorum libri sex.* Copenhagen: Ioachimus Moltkenius, 1643.

Worsaae, Jens Jacob Asmussen. *Afbildninger fra det Kongelige Museum for Nordiske Oldsager i Kjöbenhavn.* Copenhagen, 1854. New ed. as *Nordiske oldsager i det Kongelige Museum i Kjöbenhavn.* Copenhagen, 1859.

Wrenn, C. L. "Sutton Hoo and Beowulf." In *Mélanges de linguistique et de philologie Fernand Mossé in memoriam.* Paris: Didier, 1959. Pp. 495–507.

———. "Two Anglo-Saxon Harps." In Stanley B. Greenfield, ed., *Studies in Old English Literature in Honor of Arthur G. Brodeur.* Eugene: University of Oregon Books, 1963; also in *Comparative Literature* 14, no. 1 (Winter, 1962):118–128.

Zasurtsev, Pyotr Ivanovich. *Novgorod, otkrytyĭ arkheologami.* (Akademiya Nauk SSSR. Institut Arkheologii. Seriya: "Iz istorii mirovoi kul'tury.") Moscow: Izdatel'stvo "Nauka," 1967.